Grounded by Bipolar Disorder

*One Pilot's Landing*

www.brianjost.com

# Grounded by Bipolar Disorder

*One Pilot's Landing*

- A memoir

Brian Jost

Plane Paper
Publishing

ISBN  978-0-615-40659-6

10 9 8 7 6 5 4 3 2 1

Plane Paper Publishing

Printed in the United States of America

This memoir is dedicated to the people in my life who have made a difference in my recovery, including my friends, family, co-workers, health care professionals, and most of all, my wife Sarah.

# Introduction

When I am depressed, I am far below the ground, in a place where I fantasize about dying. When I am manic, I am up in the air, in the clouds, flying high. When I am stable, I am somewhere in the middle, but can easily see both up and down to those places of extreme emotion.

My insight into my psychiatric disorder has improved with each episode of depression and mania that I have experienced. However, I know that other people who have witnessed my extreme moods have had a more difficult time with trying to understand what bipolar disorder consists of and what it is like to be me as I suffer an episode of depression or mania. Although I have been told by many people that I should feel no shame concerning my disorder, I still feel the need to explain myself to those who are close to me and to others who have been confused by my unstable moods, particularly the manic episodes. While doing so, I've found that there is information in this memoir not only for my friends and my family, but for anyone whose life is touched by mental illness. There is something in this book for everyone, the people with the disorders, the psychiatrists who provide treatment, therapists, social workers, nurses, family members of people with psychiatric disorders, as well as friends and coworkers of those with mental illness. Given the prevalence of mental illness, there is no limit to the list of people who might benefit from reading this memoir.

I have stumbled upon a mission in the writing of this book. My hope is to help destroy the stigma that surrounds the topic of mental illness. I know from experience that reading and hearing the stories of other people whose lives have been touched by mental illness is a way of breaking down the barriers that exist between confusion and knowledge. With that idea in mind, I hope you enjoy my story. I also hope you share my story.

-      Brian Jost

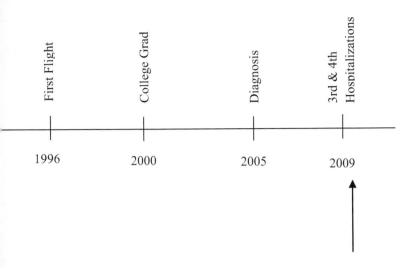

1996        2000        2005        2009

## Chapter 1 - Can We Stop For Coffee?

- Minneapolis, MN - June 9th, 2009 - Age 34 -

*- In the moment -*

Forget about the escape ladder in the back of my mind. It's gone. Someone stole it. There's nowhere to go but forward and with the speed that my mind is spinning, I won't be able to stop unless I crash.

Something is wrong. Everything feels so perfect. How can I feel this good? 2009 has been nothing but crap, yet I feel good. My job of three and a half years was taken from me. My father-in-law died. Two grad schools denied me entrance into their social work programs. My need for work is reminding me that my commercial pilot license is useless, that I am no longer medically qualified to fly…ever again. Great.

Super. Superman. I can't fly. I don't wear tights or a cape, but that's how I feel...like superman. All of these things going wrong, yet it all makes so much sense. I'm lost for words that might describe how I feel. But one word does come to mind... enlightened.

I'm turning into someone else. No. I have been someone else all along and I'm just realizing it now on this Tuesday morning. "Brian" is just a name, a cover-up to help me fit in. My thoughts are beginning to scatter. The hospital...the ER...I need to get to the ER. My wife Sarah is at work, teaching chemistry and physics at South High School in Minneapolis. I can't call her. She'll just freak out. She doesn't get it. She's never seen me like this before. If I call her I will have two problems to deal with, me and her. Let's keep it simple, I think. I'm losing control.

My two backpacks are still empty. I need to pack for the hospital. But I need to get a ride. Driving is not an option, not with me behind the wheel. I'll speed. I'll crash. I might kill someone in an accident all because of this pressure, this urgency to get to the ER and get new meds. If I had only caught this a week or two earlier, I may have been able to change meds with my psychiatrist over the phone. But now it's too late. I think I'll call Kia.

The phone is ringing and I tell myself to stay calm, talk normal, breathe...she answers. I don't need to say much. "Hey Kia...I need some help...I'm manic...I need a ride to the hospital...yeah, I'm at home...Sarah's at work." Kia says she'll be right over.  It's that simple.  No fuss, no worries.  She's a level-headed doctor.  She'll be cool about it.  Now it's time to fill those two backpacks.

Sweat pants will be good to have in the hospital.  They're comfortable.  Plus I don't want to wear the aqua colored pants they hand out at Fairview, not because of the color, but because I don't want to look like everyone else.  I take the tie string out of the waist of the pants.  There's no way I'll be allowed to have the string.  I might hang myself with it, or strangle someone.  No, I don't want to do those things, but the hospital staff has their rules.  Belts are not allowed for the same reason.  I want something to write on while I'm in the hospital and find a couple spiral bound notebooks, but they won't let me have those, not with the wire in them.  Continuing to dig, I find a different notepad without a wire.  I continue packing… clothes, books, medication, nutritional supplements, some snacks, almonds, walnuts, blueberries, and grapes.  Hospital food is awful.

My suspicion that I am not Brian is growing stronger.  I have stumbled upon a well kept secret.  I feel special, very special.  In fact, I believe I may have been chosen.  They will know at the hospital that I am not the average lunatic.  Perhaps they will allow me to have the tie string in my sweat pants and my belt and my spiral bound notebooks.  I'll still leave those items behind for now, but I'm thinking they will put me somewhere in the hospital where I don't need to stick to the rules.

OK, I'm running out of time. I have something big to take care of. My wife still thinks I am just Brian, but soon people will find out who I really am. When that happens, I will be wanted by many groups of people, both good and evil. I can feel the miraculous events that I will be part of. Prison. I will be put in prison. It will appear as if I have done something wrong, but I know that at least in prison I will have protection. But I'll still need proof of who I really am, who I have become, or who I have been all this time. I have proof and I need to give it to my wife. Then she'll be able to tell the people who I am.

The answer and the proof of who I am is in my journals, my home videos, my email exchanges with people throughout the years, my songs that I have written and recorded, and also on computer hard-drives. All of these items are in four small locked fire-proof safes. It's time now to give my wife access to all of these things. She'll need the proof. Two of the safes have digital codes. The other two need keys. I leave the codes and keys on my desk along with usernames and passwords for several email accounts. Just like I am not going to tell Kia who I am, I can't simply leave a note for Sarah telling her who I am. Instead, I leave a note next to the keys, codes, and passwords that reads "Just keep digging. You'll find the story." Shit, Sarah's going to flip when she sees this. I know it won't make sense to her right away. I guess it will just have to unfold as time passes.

Connections are firing in my brain, piecing together years of events that I used to think were just coincidences, but now look to be part of a larger plan. Who am I? Who have I become? There is something beautiful happening. Questions pop into my mind. My life has brought me full circle to make me who I am today.

I don't understand it, but I am picking up some new information seemingly out of thin air. It is confirmed, I have been chosen. I can't explain it yet, and I know it is complicated. But definitely, I am chosen, and absolutely I am not just Brian. I can't tell anyone. That would be too risky. If I tell anyone, I will be viewed as being completely crazy. People might think that my mind is in so much disarray that I could become harmful to myself or others. Telling Kia is not an option, at least not yet. It's crucial that I leave home acting as myself as much as possible and I must convince myself that I am still just me. That's impossible. OK, I'll be me, but I'll let it remain on some deeper level that I will soon prove to be someone else.

That's it. I'm packed, ready to go. I grab my filled water bottle from the fridge, lock my condo door and head outside to wait for Kia. Sarah's going to be pissed. I still haven't called her. She doesn't know that I'm going to the ER. She'll probably hate that I called Kia for a ride. But considering what is happening to me, I just need to worry about myself. Kia and I go back to '93 with the line between being friends and more than friends blurry in my mind at times, but all I need from her on this day is an unbiased, peaceful ride to the ER.

Kia and her three year old son Hank arrive and I climb into the suburban. She asks "Can we stop for coffee on the way?" I must look more relaxed than I feel. "That's fine with me" I say, and we're off. There's still a little time. I'm losing control, but I'm keeping it together at the same time. We pull up to the drive-through window at Starbucks, Kia pays for her drink and the barista hands Kia a newspaper free of charge and without a request for the paper. The man says "A little education for you..." I'm sure he's looking me in the eye. This must be yesterday's paper. Taking the paper from Kia, I glance at the front page and see an article that has something to do with a man going on a big adventure. This is another message for me.

It's time to breathe now and I rest my head against the seat. "Do you want to go to Fairview?" Kia asks. Definitely, I want to go to Fairview. I'm feeling a little more pressured now. My mind is splitting apart, I know it. I can feel it. It's happening faster. We'll make it in time, but we're cutting it close now. The ride through Minneapolis is easy and we arrive at the hospital.

"Should I just drop you off at the ER and then I can park and come in?" Kia asks. Yes, I tell her and I grab my backpacks and walk into my refuge. I'm calm on the outside. I'm good at this. I think about how I should have been an actor. Maybe I missed my calling. I present an appearance of peacefulness.

Sitting down with the intake person, I provide my name, Brian, which is not what I have come to believe is my real name. We go through all of the paper work and discuss medications. I get to wear an ID wrist band. I'm done checking in. By this time Kia and Hank are inside with me. A drastic change kicks in. I almost fall over.

I'm reminded of my brother and me playing with sparklers at night on the fourth of July as kids. Watching my brother write his name in the air with the burning wire in the dark, K-E-V-I-N, the streaks of light trail behind the movement of the sparkler. There's a streak of light that the sparkler forgot to take with it. I'm seeing streaks of light now in the ER. But this is different. It starts with watching Hank play with toys in the waiting room. Streaks of light shoot away from his face, hands, and his whole body as he moves. But the light is moving away from his body before he moves. His body is following the light, not the other way around. I'm seeing the streaks of light as an indication of where Hank is about to be, so I reason that I am seeing the future. I get dizzy and I have to sit down.

Doing my best to be still, I am patiently waiting for someone to come get me and take me to an ER room. I'm still dizzy, although if I close my eyes I feel a little more stable. A nurse calls me out of the waiting room. I stand and walk towards her. Kia and Hank follow. I look around at everyone:

Kia, Hank, the nurse, and a couple other people walking down a hall. Streaks of light lead each of them along their paths. I see all of their futures and everyone is obeying their destiny. This is a comfort to me. This tells me we all belong somewhere and even if we don't know why we are going the way we are, we are supposed to go there. But I'm not so sure I want to see the future. I stumble behind the nurse as she leads me to my room.

I'm in a room with a bed that is smaller than a twin bed, but nothing else, no chair for Kia to sit on. I sit on the bed. She stands. Hank walks around the room looking for something to do, but finds nothing. A security guard stands outside of the room looking in at me through the single window. This is cool. I've checked into the ER before, but I've never had my own security guard. He looks friendly.

I'm losing it. We barely made it here in time. There are flashes of images, visions, creeping into my head, things I don't want to see. These are images from the future. They must be because they are real and I know they are not from the past or present. It goes back and forth between seeing the room I'm in and the visions of the future. I can't watch. This information is not meant to be known. I close my eyes and the images get stronger. It's time to start pacing, and I make a couple circles that go by the door. The security guard moves into the doorway. He still looks friendly, but now he looks a little more engaged in his job.

The images are moving faster. I can't keep up with them. I sit back down on the bed and hold my head in my hands. I see a quick vision of my wife dying in a car crash, just her face. She is calm, peaceful. She's gone. I wonder if she knew I was in the hospital and then I think that maybe this accident just happened. Maybe she left work to be with me and now she is dead. I can't make sense of it. I know I haven't called Sarah yet, and I don't think Kia has called her, not yet. Or has she? This must be the future I am seeing. Sarah is going to visit her father. She will go home to be with him. Maybe that's why she dies. Maybe they need to be with each other.

An image of a nuclear explosion fills my head. It's all I can see, a huge mushroom cloud. I'm just a few miles away from it. It's orange and yellow and filled with fire and rage. I feel the destruction. Kia's husband, Dave, is there. This must be Afghanistan. My vision stops and in its place is a storm of knowledge. I receive a message that Dave will die in the war. But it is not sad. I know that Dave is a crucial part of an urgent upcoming attack and the attack will only be successful if he is a part of it. Dave is an angel, a warrior angel. He will be part of ending the wars.

Kia says "It's going to be alright." I say "I know." It's time for Kia to leave. She rounds up Hank and makes her way out of the room.

My sense of peace with these future events disappears. Even though I can find understanding behind

13

death, I am not ready to lose Sarah. Kia is not ready to lose Dave. Hank is not ready to lose his father. These things cannot happen. I will not let them happen. Struggling with my mind, I know there must be a way to change the future. It's not as simple as wishing or trying to will something different to happen. I must go back to the beginning, back in time, back to when there was nothing but God. One step at a time, I think to myself. It's time to go back in time and create a different path of events so that the visions of the future I saw will not come true.

Standing up, I begin to walk backwards, pacing step by step in a backwards circle. Concentrating intensely, I know I must undo everything I have ever known, everything that has made me who I am. Every drop of my attention is focused inside my mind. A vision presents itself. It's me. I have it locked in now, the vision of me who will go back in time. Now it's like I'm watching a movie. The friendly looking security guard steps out of the doorway. I walk backwards from the room to the waiting room where I see Hank playing with the toys in reverse. A ball rolls, then bounces along the floor towards him and hops up off the ground, landing in his hands. He runs backwards. I move in reverse to the check-in desk. Kia and Hank walk backwards out the ER, going to the parked suburban. My wrist band is removed. The pen in my hands sucks the ink off the documents as I un-sign my name. Step by step, I walk backwards out of the ER and get into Kia's car. The entire city of Minneapolis moves in reverse as we make our way back to my condo. It's working. I am going back in time.

My focus becomes distracted. Someone has made a mistake. I've been manic before, but never like this. This is the first time I have seen the future. This is the first time I have seen streaks of light leading people along their paths. The messages I have been receiving, that is new also. They were wrong, the doctors, in 2005. I'm hallucinating. My thinking is delusional. This is something more than just bipolar disorder. This is schizophrenia. This must be schizophrenia. "Focus," I tell myself. I jump back into my mindset of going back in time. It's time to save some lives.

Step by step, I have to take apart my life, disassemble the pieces until there is nothing left but the beginning. Then I will rebuild. All of my memories must be destroyed, all of my cares forgotten. In my head I have to move backwards, taking away the good and the bad. Highlights run through my head.

The first image that shows up concerns my mania in 2006. I see myself in Rod & Gun Park in Eau Claire, Wisconsin and I am smoking a joint with a woman who I just met in the parking lot. My euphoria allows me to connect with her soul and after talking with her for about 20 minutes we hug goodbye. Circumstances bring police officers to pick me up and take me to the hospital because of my mania and perhaps because of my bad reaction to the marijuana. I have a video recorder with me, and feeling like the world's most important documentarian, I make sure the camera is rolling throughout my manic episode in the parking lot of the park. I ask the police to handcuff me so that I don't startle them. It's probably all in my head, but I feel extremely jumpy and I am certain that my tender nerves will cause a reaction by the officers that will send a bullet through my innocent flesh. I'm just not sure if they know how to handle me.

I pop out of that memory. Other memories flash before my eyes such as the short lived intense relationships that accompany mania. There's the woman I thought I would marry even though we spent only a few nights together. I guess there has been more than one of those relationships. With splendid pain I think of another woman whose name I can't even recall. It's so easy to fall in love when I'm manic.

There is also the memory of skydiving while manic and the recollection of a friend calling the police when she learned that I would be jumping out of a plane. She was certain that I would conveniently forget to pull my ripcord.

Another memory shows up, that of receiving the diagnosis of bipolar disorder in 2005 and the accompanying feeling of intelligence concerning learning something about myself that requires great confidence to acknowledge. And of course another memory is tied to the diagnosis, that of losing my right to exercise my commercial pilot privileges. My mind goes to memories such as my first training flight and my first solo flight. Those are memories that will never die, and they bring about many images of my experiences flying all over the country. I think about all the places I moved for flying jobs,

Spokane, Fairbanks, South Dakota, and Minnesota. Thinking about moving in general makes me think of moving for other reasons, for education and relationships, which makes me think of Florida where I went to school for music and audio recording arts.

Florida makes me think of the stripper that I nearly accidentally married. She reminds me of other relationships that didn't work out, and that takes me out of the hospital and drops me into different parts of Washington, Oregon, North Dakota, South Carolina, and other parts of the country.

The fact that I lived so many places makes me think of all the friends I have made over the years and certain people stand out. There is Blake who I met in Orlando. He invited me to attend a church that sucked me into a dangerous battle between God and Satan. I seemed to be stuck in the middle of this battle. There is another guy I met in Orlando, Pat. He and I were together when I felt the electric current of evil pass through my body moments before a strange man not far from us, a man we did not even know was there, fired a pistol that made us run and place an urgent call to the police. Pat also felt something just before the gun was fired, so I know it's not all just in my head.

I think about how Pat, Blake, and a guy named Peter, made up the worship band at the church. Then I think of how those guys invited me to join the worship band. That's when Satan started fucking with me, splitting my mind in two.

17

Memories show up out of order. The depressions present themselves, the times when I no longer wanted to live, the times when I dreamed of ways to die. The suicide plans that have never fully disappeared show a little brighter now.

I think about the faces I saw on the bathroom wall of an apartment in Aberdeen, South Dakota. I was being watched. Another memory comes from Aberdeen, a memory of a woman in church speaking in tongues. That was the day I thought I would never go to church again.

All of my drinking surfaces into my memory. I remember the alcohol that numbed the pain that I didn't even realize I was experiencing. Although I can't forget the taste, the altered state of mind is what I recall the most and is also what I still miss.

Clearly I am spending too much time on these memories. I must go back in time faster and I begin to skip years of my life, years that might not matter if I am able to go back and create a different future. As I reach my younger years, the speed at which I am moving backwards in time becomes immeasurable, seemingly as fast as the speed of light at certain points, skipping through years of unimportant events and growth. Before I know it, I am backed up to when I was just a baby and it becomes time for me to become unborn.

I lie down on the bed in the room and close my eyes, resting quietly on my back. All I see is white. I feel that I will experience the death of my body without truly dying, and that my spirit will rise in the form of my unborn self in order to continue back in time all the way to Jesus' time as a man on Earth. I believe that if my spirit is allowed to die, I will be able to become the spirit of Jesus. I allow these things to happen, to let my body die, then my spirit. I am now Jesus, and as Jesus I am still going back in time. Returning to life, I find myself on a cross, crucified, but I feel no pain. I understand that I must continue to go back in time and I do so, going all the way back to the birth of Jesus, now my birth. I am now unborn, and I rise as God. I am God. But I am confused. Standing now, I turn to the security guard and say "I am God?" It's both a statement and a question, as I am not sure what is going on. Then, "Am I God?" Next, "You are God...? We are God? We are all God? We are all God. This is Heaven? I'm in Heaven? Is this Heaven?" Then it happens.

Feeling like a bird, I see images from above. I see people on their knees with their heads bowed forward on the ground. This is true praise, true worship. I see flashes of people all over the world in similar poses. Some are chanting. Some are praying out loud. Most are silent. The wars were filled with evil, but now there is world peace. I see it coming.

I realize that I have become very, very intelligent, acquiring much information about war, plans of terrorist attacks, and all sorts of information concerning The United States' national security. I know immediately that I have to speak face to face with President Obama.

I am given a heavy dose of medication, an anti-psychotic. The next thing I know, my body is in a wheel chair, but my spirit floats about three feet in front of my body. I can see myself, a view from the front as if I am staring face to face with myself. Clearly, I am not in my body. I am being pushed in the chair to a different part of the hospital, as a room has finally been prepared for my stay. The anti-psychotic is making me feel like I am about to pass-out, and I experience a brief meeting with the President. I see my arm outstretched toward Mr. Obama as we shake hands with great strength and great trust. As we shake hands, the power of God that I have within me is transferred to the President. We salute each other and he abruptly turns away, walking with intention to carry out his patriotic duties with the new information he has just acquired. Sensing that my mission is complete, I lose the last bit of any energy and pass out onto the floor.

*To be continued in Chapter 3...*

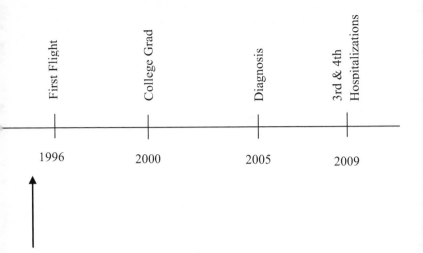

First Flight

College Grad

Diagnosis

3rd & 4th Hospitalizations

1996          2000          2005          2009

**Chapter 2:  First Flight and Before**

- Duluth, MN - 1993 to 1996 - Ages 18 to 21 -

- Looking back -

My aviation career can be traced back to high school, my senior year, having taken an introduction to aviation class. There was no actual flying involved, just the basics of navigation, aerodynamics, FAA rules and regulations. The idea of being a pilot seemed cool, but not realistic for me. I didn't have the self confidence required to take on a dream like that. At that point I had already been accepted into the University of Minnesota, Duluth (UMD) and after high school graduation I continued with that route. However, the idea of becoming a pilot found a place in the back of my mind, and it slowly became an unreachable dream that I carried with me into my first years of college.

My time at UMD seemed to have been a lost cause in some ways. I switched majors from business to mechanical engineering to biology, finally realizing that I was technically "undecided." At 20 I transferred from UMD to attend Lake Superior College (LSC) in Duluth, having enrolled in a computer-aided drafting program. My idea of transferring to LSC for drafting stemmed from a couple of years of drafting classes in high school. Although not terribly exciting, I found drafting to be interesting and a good use of my attention to detail. But I lasted only one quarter at LSC. After getting all A's that quarter, I dropped out when I realized I wasn't really into the program. That was the first time I felt truly lost with my life, not knowing what to do or where to go, and that's when I decided I had no reason to not try flying. The idea had been in my head ever since my high school senior year, and now more than three years later, it was finally time to do something about it. I went to a small airport in nearby Superior, Wisconsin and inquired about what it takes to become a pilot.

An older man, Bill, took me up in a small two-seater. After getting us in the air he handed the controls over to me and I was flying for the first time. I banked left and right, I climbed, descended, and adjusted the power. Flying felt natural to me. I was meant to do it. It hit me that I would do this for a career. I was up there with the clouds and I didn't want to come down. The bird's-eye view of the city fed my ego, making me feel like I was in charge of everything below me. I was King on that day, on that first flight. Enough of the city, I thought, and headed northeast along the northern shoreline of Lake Superior away from Duluth. I told Bill that I wanted to see the Lakeview Castle, a restaurant on the shore about ten miles out of Duluth where I had been working as a waiter, and he told me to show him the way. I maneuvered our plane directly over the restaurant then banked right, over the water, to get a better view, and descended enough to see the front of the restaurant. There it was, the Lakeview Castle, the place where I often talked to my coworkers about my dream of flying. It looked like such a lonely place, stuck on the ground with no wings like mine.

I took us back to the airport and Bill talked me through the approach and even had me make my first radio calls, announcing our position and intentions to any traffic in the area. His hands and feet were at the ready, prepared to take control if I were to get us in an unusual attitude or headed in the wrong direction. On our final approach Bill told me what to expect in the landing and continued to talk me through the most exciting part of the flight. The landing was rough, but we were on the ground. Bill claimed that he didn't need to touch the controls the whole way down. He said I nailed the approach airspeeds and that I was a smooth flyer. I wasn't so sure he was telling the truth.

The King had landed. I bought a logbook and made the flight official. I was hooked and there was no turning back. The next five months I worked as a waiter at three restaurants and built up flight time towards getting a private pilot certificate. Anxiously, I waited to begin the four-year aviation program at the University of North Dakota, UND, in Grand Forks to begin in the upcoming fall. I was looking forward to the new adventure.

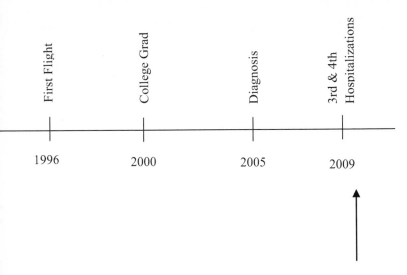

First Flight

College Grad

Diagnosis

3rd & 4th Hospitalizations

|————————|————————|————————|————————————

1996            2000            2005            2009

## Chapter 3:  The Conductor

- Minneapolis, MN - June, 2009 - Age 34 -

*- In the moment -*

***Continued from chapter 1****: Then, sensing that my mission is complete, I lose the last bit of any energy and pass out onto the floor.*

When I wake, my wife Sarah and my new psychiatrist are in my room.  I am on the floor, half in the bathroom, half out.  I am struggling to stand, but just can't do it.  With the help of my wife and the doctor, I am able to get off the floor and into a chair.  The doctor is holding a clip board in front of me with a release of information form that he wants me to sign giving the hospital the OK to give Sarah my medical records. He holds the form in front of me and asks me to sign it, but I am not responding well at all. Everything is very foggy and his voice seems to echo, as if I am observing the past just a second or so after things are actually happening. Or perhaps I just bounced back into the near future and that is the cause of the echoes. Either way, I am not responding well to the requests to sign the release form, not because I don't want to sign it, but because I seem to lack the strength to move. The doctor keeps repeating his request for me to sign and places a pen in my right hand. I have no control over my hand or arm. I want my arm to move, and it finally does, but it is not under my control. It's like I am watching someone else move my arm for me, as if I'm just a puppet. I watch my arm slowly reach for the paper and my hand signs on the line in capital letters "GOD." My wife asks the doctor if that counts, and apparently it is good enough. Next comes the date. Again, I am not responding so well. I think that it is June 10th, the day after Kia brought me to the ER, but it turns out I am wrong, and in fact it is still the same day, June 9th. The doctor repeats the date, prompting me to sign the form. Finally I write just the number 9 on the form in the blank for the date. And there it is, "GOD – 9," so simple and so pure. The hospital staff would no longer have to guess who I have become.

It's still day one in Fairview hospital, evening, June 9th 2009. My wife Sarah has just left the hospital and I'm on my own now, but not really. There are many people who will help me. It's just a matter of piecing it all together. There are so many things happening at once and making sense of everything is difficult. Knowing that people will help me feels good, just like it feels good to know that I will help people everywhere. President Obama is on my mind. Thinking about the encounter I had with him around the time I passed out from the antipsychotic medication, I understand that I did not meet him in the way that two people usually meet in this world. I understand that nobody else witnessed our meeting. Just as I knew my visions of nuclear war and world peace were visions of future events, I now understand that my vision of meeting with President Obama is a vision of the future. But I can't wait around and just hope it happens. I must make it happen. It was a vision of what must happen in the future. If I am to meet with President Obama, I will need to leave the hospital. Or maybe I can find a way to bring the President to me. I am too exhausted to focus on what I must do. My brain was just put through the ringer today while receiving the visions of the future. I must rest. A staff member comes into my room and gives me a folder filled with information about my stay at the hospital. Setting the folder on the nightstand, I choose to sleep.

My eyes open and everything is clear to me. It's morning, day two in the hospital. They've been waiting for someone like me to show up. They've been waiting for change and now it's here. The answers to all their questions are about to overtake them as they wait patiently in awe and wonder. It's the doctors who have been waiting, the psychiatrists and psychologists. These people have a lot to learn from me, but it will not be an easy task to share everything I know with them. There are so many of them, doctors from all over the world, all receiving the word that I have arrived at Fairview hospital in Minneapolis. All of these professionals will need to study me so they can go back to where they came from and spread my knowledge. They know that only the best of them will be allowed in the hospital with me, to study me and learn from me. Their numbers will be limited, but still it will be like conducting an orchestra. Yes, I will be the conductor, and they will each bring a unique instrument, and together we will make beautiful music. Together we will make a change in the mental health system. Together we will prove that mental illness is a gift, not a curse, and in the end we will destroy the stigma that surrounds mental illness. I can't wait to get started.

Opening the folder on the nightstand, I read about my rights as a patient, and see that there are some forms for me to fill out. One form asks for me to list and rate my symptoms that I am experiencing. I set the forms at the foot of my bed and sit facing out the window of my room. I have the room to myself. This is a major advantage. I know from experience that some rooms have three beds in them. This is just a small indication that they have caught on, that I am not like everyone else. They definitely know I need special treatment. Or at least I hope they know. I begin to doubt my knowledge, not the truth behind my knowledge, but the timing of it. Perhaps I still need to prove to them that I need special treatment. Maybe doctors from all over the world are not yet on their way to Fairview. Maybe I need to ask them to come first.

People need me. I know all the secrets of how to end the wars. All of this intelligence that I have is a direct result of my mental illness. I know that I received the wrong diagnosis four years ago, and that really I have schizophrenia, not bipolar disorder. That explains the hallucinations, the delusions of reference and my visions of the future. It is this mental illness that has allowed me to experience these things. A gift from God is what this illness is. Clearly, I have been chosen to be a messenger, to be someone who passes along information from God to those who need the information. Yes, it is a gift, this mental illness.

I am now living proof that there are benefits to having a mental illness. In fact, I am living proof that mental illness really isn't an illness at all. Rather, it is a misunderstood phenomenon. It is a result of God speaking and communicating on a level that most people cannot comprehend. God has chosen me to prove that mental illness is what will help save the world from war and destruction. Without this so-called mental illness, this so-called bipolar disorder, or what I now know is this so-called schizophrenia, I would not have the tendency for my mind to drift into other dimensions and receive messages from God. This is the opportunity of a lifetime. Cooperation on my part with the doctors is a must to learn how all of this happened to me. I am ready to work with them, ready to be their guinea pig.

I must fill out this form about my symptoms, so I open the folder that I placed at the foot of my bed. Filling out the form as completely as possible, I make sure to list the symptoms that are new to me, the hallucinations, delusions of reference, delusional thinking. I write in the margin of the form "It's schizophrenia, not bipolar disorder," and I underline it, circle it, and add a star and an exclamation point for emphasis. Clearly, if I am able to be aware of these symptoms, then it must mean that I am OK, and that I can use these symptoms to my benefit and to the benefit of the world. But I can't do a whole lot of good to anyone while I am stuck here in the hospital. There must be a way out of here. I look over the form and double-check the list of symptoms I have written. I don't want to miss anything. I have heard that many people with mental illness try to hide things from their doctors. Not me. I want the doctors to know everything. The truth, the whole truth, nothing but the truth. A simple and obvious instruction, I write on the form "We need to get the team together from round one." The doctors will understand that they will have to contact the doctors that I worked with during my first major manic episode and diagnosis four years earlier in September 2005. The form is complete. Now I need to find a way of getting the attention of the hospital staff so I can conduct the orchestra.

## Day Two in Fairview – The 1st Breakfast

In my room, I pull the thin blanket off my bed and lay it out on the floor. Then I rest on the floor on my back, legs laid straight and I pray. As I pray I also communicate with my friend Blake. He's the guy I came to know well in Florida while going to school for music recording. He knows that I have attained the power of God and that I have the power to make great prophecies. Knowing in my heart that Blake has been reached by the FBI because of his connections with me, I pray silently to him in order to communicate my need to leave the hospital. I am surprised that I am still here. A nurse comes into my room while I am still on the floor to tell me breakfast has arrived. Now I realize that the hospital staff is required to run me through the usual process of treatment without skipping any official steps. It seems they know I have to get out, but they have to keep me until the official paperwork can be completed, documenting my successful treatment which will show that I am healthy and stable. I figure this will take only a couple hours since it is a matter of national security that I be let out of the hospital. So I start playing the game, trying to go along with everything that is asked of me.

The huge silver, metal cart full of breakfast trays is sitting near the main staff desk. There's a line of patients waiting impatiently for their food. I stand back behind all of them and take on a pose of indifference. There may not be enough food for me to get any. I'll wait and see if everyone else gets a breakfast tray. If there is anything left over, I will take the food. But I could skip breakfast. Given all the strength, power, and energy that is flowing into my body from another world, I'm not sure I even need food.

Everyone gets their breakfast and there is a tray left at the end for me. There is even a sheet of paper on the tray with my name on it. Slowly grabbing the tray, I look for a place to sit. All of the patients are scattered about in the common area. A group sits in front of the TV. I don't want to watch TV, and I don't want to sit next to anyone, mostly because I don't belong here. These people, the patients, are not ready to be near me. I have much to do, and much to say, but little of that will be with the patients on the unit. I must work with the doctors and staff to get out of here so I can begin my mission. The patients here cannot help me.

Finding a seat that is not next to anyone else, I take a close look at my tray and see two hard boiled eggs, a small bowl of sliced peaches and hash browns. I don't need the hash browns or peaches, but I should probably get a little protein in me, so I eat the eggs. I do not speak while I eat. It does not take long to eat the eggs, and almost as soon as I start, I am finished and walking back to my room. I need to meditate and pray. I need to communicate with my team members.

With the door to my room closed, I leave the window curtain open. There is a view of trees and a river. It's a pretty good view for being in a hospital. I experienced the same view four years ago here in Fairview when I was diagnosed with bipolar disorder. I sit on the edge of my bed, facing the window with my legs crossed. I do not take the common pose for meditation. Instead, I allow my head to fall forward and let my arms dangle down in front of me, hanging along the side of the bed. Taking a deep breath, I let my body go limp, but I don't fall over. I am in the perfect position. There are distractions from outside my bedroom door. I tell them to go away, to be silenced, and they are turned off like a light switch. I am gone, in another world. Peace surrounds me. Hearing helicopters in the distance, I can tell they are approaching the hospital. How many are there? I am not sure, but I know they are coming for me. One of these helicopters carries President Obama. He is approaching with his team. They need me to join them. They need to use my knowledge, my intelligence, and my ability to decipher secret messages. They are getting closer. They will be here soon.

Lifting my arms, I hold them out in front of me, then make motions with my arms that tell the helicopter pilots to keep coming in towards me. "Come on in, come on" I repeat in my head. I wait. They arrive at the hospital. I can now sense that there are at least six helicopters. They are right outside the front of the hospital. Only one helicopter lands. The pilot keeps the engine running while eight men get out and walk into the hospital. They are secret service. The rest of the helicopters continue to hover at about 50 feet above the ground. President Obama's helicopter is one that is hovering. They will continue to hover until the secret service brings me outside. Then President Obama's helicopter will land. I sense that the President will step out of the helicopter to meet me, to shake my hand. Then he and I will climb into the helicopter and depart to fight the necessary wars. I wait. I am patient. Soon I will be gone.

I know that I will be gone for three years. That's how long it will take, this mission that I am going on, although I have no details as to why it will be three years versus any other length. My wife and family will miss me. At first they will not understand what has happened to me or why I am gone. But the government will brief them on my whereabouts. My family will not be told everything about my mission, just that I have critical information about the wars and about terrorists and that the President needs me to work with our government. My family will not be told how long this mission will take.

Something distracts me. I lose my focus on the world outside of the hospital and all that is going on with the helicopters. Exhaustion is all I feel and the light from the window is too much to handle. After closing the curtain, I lay down in my bed and get under the covers. I think about how I will be going away from my wife and the rest of my family and friends and it makes me sad. I cry. I cry hard. But I don't cry for long. The mission makes sense to me and I understand that I must accept the circumstances that I am in. Getting out of bed, I open the curtains. I can't hear the

helicopters.  I must have just heard and sensed the future.  The
helicopters will come.  They are just not here yet.

*To be continued in Chapter 5...*

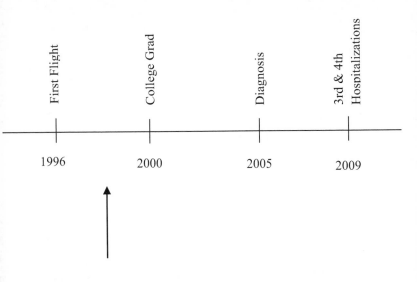

First Flight

College Grad

Diagnosis

3rd & 4th Hospitalizations

1996          2000          2005          2009

## Chapter 4:  Wings and Music
- Grand Forks, ND  - 1996 to 2000 - Ages 21 to 25 -
- Looking Back -

Writing about my time at UND in Grand Forks, North Dakota is difficult because those four years were filled with happiness and excitement about life.  It hurts to remember the good times and those four years were the best four years of my life.  I had a lot going for me back then.  Friends were everywhere I turned.  The aviation program was building me up to be a professional pilot.  I was in love.  Life was wonderful, and I had no doubts about myself, no fears or anxieties.  Life was different back then.  It was close to perfect.  Often I try to forget those four years, but without the memory of my time at UND, I would have nothing to strive for with my mental health. I need those memories to use as a marker. Those memories represent where it is I am trying to get back to in terms of my happiness, health, and well-being. Those memories contain the feelings and emotions that I want and need to experience again. I just can't let go of the good times for fear of forgetting where it is that I need to go and what it is that I need to do.

Those four years at UND can be broken down into a few basic parts of life... relationships, flying, music, and partying. I'll start with relationships. Almost as soon as I arrived to the University of North Dakota I met 12 people who I thought I would remain friends with forever. At the time, I didn't think about what would happen four years later after we all graduated. I didn't consider that one of the group members might leave UND to move home to Chicago, or that another member of the group might not feel that he was in the right place at the right time and that he should move home to Colorado. And I just didn't consider that all of my friends might scatter around the country after graduation. Looking back at my time at UND, it hurts to know that these 12 people are no longer in my life.

It wasn't so important that I was a commercial pilot in training, but it was important that I was pursuing a passion. It's not the fact that I knew how to fly that was important, but that I knew how to pursue the goal of learning how to fly. I recognize now that I had a dream, a huge dream, and even though that dream at first seemed too large to tackle, I found ways to break it apart into smaller goals, little steps along the way to reaching the final destination. Being surrounded by other people who were pursuing the same dream as me helped me to keep the momentum. If one of us began to slip in making progress, the others would grab hold and pull that person back in line with their intentions. People are what made up those four years for me. Relationships are what kept me motivated. I was in love with life and so excited about where I might be headed, that I never even noticed that I might have a drinking problem. Well, not until about two months prior to graduation.

After four years of education at UND, I went on a date with someone new to me. We were to go out for dinner, then meet up with some friends at a comedy club. I told her at the beginning of the night that if we ended up having too much to drink, that one of my friends could drive us home because he never drank. She caught on before I did that I started the evening with intentions of getting drunk. Although I can't recall her words, I can recall the feeling that I got from her response when I told her we had a sober driver for the night. It was a feeling of a brick being thrown at my head. It was a feeling of "wake up, dummy." It was a feeling of doubt, as I wondered if I was doing something wrong. And it was a feeling of being a lowly person, a feeling of shame. That night was at the end of my four years of UND, and not once before that did I think I had a drinking problem. I just thought

I was like everyone else, having fun, going to parties, and getting drunk with friends. The experience was not strong enough to make me stop drinking. I continued to need the altered state of mind.

There were at least twelve of us that met almost immediately upon arrival at UND in the fall of 1996. All of us were new to UND. Most of us were transfer students. We clicked so quickly that we didn't even see it happening. I don't know what it is that is different now that makes it feel impossible to ever click with a group of people like that again. I want to make new friends again.

Maybe the difference is that I am married. Is that it? That shouldn't be the reason. In fact, that would just be an excuse. It's probably more about my life feeling muted. It's partly the medication, partly the stigma, and partly because I often feel exhausted from trying so hard to take care of myself. Sometimes I feel like I just don't have time for other people, and often I feel like I don't want to be with anyone else. I often find myself more comfortable alone.

It's mostly my fault that I don't have many friends anymore. Sometimes I blame my psychiatric disorder. But although bipolar disorder can truthfully cause a rift between people, it's still up to me to do something about it. I can't expect a friend to just be OK with my disorder without some explanation. It's like I did something wrong to a friend, something disrespectful, and now I need to offer an apology, an explanation of why I did whatever it was that I did. But with bipolar disorder I shouldn't have to offer an apology, just an explanation. The apologies still surface though, because the disorder brings to life many actions and words that deserve a request for forgiveness. As far as the explanation goes, that usually feels like a task most likely unachievable. For me, the person with the disorder, it has taken years to understand, and for a friend to understand bipolar disorder will take even longer. I can't even expect that other person to understand my situation until I understand my situation, and then it is up to me to reach out and try to help that friend take a look at me and see that I am still here, somewhere inside, maybe hiding a little, wanting to come out and play.

I'm not close with my old friends from UND anymore. I want to be close to them but everything has changed. I want my past back. It's not so much that I want to go back and do anything different. I just want to go back and stay there, get stuck in the best years of my life. I miss my friends.

I am trying to get used to all the change that has accompanied the diagnosis of bipolar disorder. I'm trying to get used to the fact that I started to lose relationships after I was diagnosed. I am trying to get used to the fact that my passions have been altered. Not being able to fly is a no-brainer. It's written out in black and white in the FAA rules and regulations. With the diagnosis of bipolar disorder, I simply cannot get an aviation medical certificate. But there is also the lost passion of music.

It started right after I arrived at UND in the fall of 1996. A friend let me borrow his guitar, my first experience with a musical instrument. The sound waves that vibrated from the guitar captivated my senses with an intense calm that put my mind in a trance. Instantly, I was hooked on music, and while I would continue the aviation program for four years, I would spend much of my free time teaching myself to play the guitar by ear, writing and recording songs alone or with a friend. Dreams of becoming an audio engineer crept into my head, at times overpowering my urge to take to the sky. But I did not stray from my goal of finding work as a pilot.

I met another friend in Grand Forks, Josh. He also played the guitar and couldn't help but to write songs when he wasn't flying. We spent a lot of time together working on music, recording songs, and thinking that maybe we would be in a band some day. Maybe the truth is that he didn't think we would be in a real band someday, but the idea of starting a band certainly grew in my mind.

You might wonder how music can be taken from a person. Perhaps it isn't music specifically, but maybe the change in my creativity. It's the medication that I blame. I've heard from other people that medication can numb creativity. Some say that isn't true, but I think it is. There is something different about my brain on meds compared to being clean of meds. Before I was medicated, music was in me, and I was able to let it out, turn it into songs as I played the guitar and sang, making recordings of what was pouring out of me. I've recorded over 300 songs over the years, but now, although the music is still inside me, I am unable to let it out. It's trapped in my head and heart. I can feel it and hear it, but I can't turn it into actual sound. I still appreciate music and listen to music as much as possible. Often, I listen to my iPod when I get into bed. Different types of music can help to adjust my mood. So, I haven't lost my love for music. It's just that I have lost the ability to take the music that is inside my head and turn it into something useful. It's like I'm trying to broadcast music from within, but someone is jamming the signal. It's there. I can feel it. It just can't get out.

When the end of my four-year degree arrived, I was itching to leave North Dakota, looking forward to a new adventure. My time at UND had been wonderful, but it was time to find something new, and I began my job search a couple months before graduation.

My heart told me to go west, but I did look for work around Minneapolis because of a woman who I had recently started dating. We didn't have much time together, but I did consider wanting to be near where she lived in Minneapolis. But I wasn't able to find a suitable flight job. And at that point, the only job I would have taken was a flight job. Plus I have to acknowledge the urge I had within me to just leave, to just pick up and go somewhere completely different.

Just a couple weeks before commencement, I was offered a flight instructor position in Spokane, Washington. I was so ready for the new job that I left Grand Forks soon after taking my last final exam, skipping my graduation ceremony. I was headed west. My career had arrived.

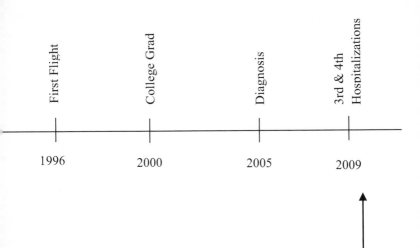

First Flight

College Grad

Diagnosis

3rd & 4th Hospitalizations

1996          2000          2005          2009

## Chapter 5:  Letting Go

- Minneapolis, MN - June, 2009 - Age 34 -

*- In the moment -*

**Continued from chapter 3:** *.   I must have just heard and sensed the future.   The helicopters will come.   They just are not here yet.*

It feels like day two in Fairview Hospital still, but I know it's been longer.  Time is compressing into an endless moment and I can no longer keep track here in the hospital. However, I am still aware of my past and future.  Since I know I will soon be leaving my loved ones behind to work with the President on stopping the wars, it is time to start letting go of my past. I can sense that my mission will be exhausting and that my mind and soul will be intensely taxed to the point of near death. It is difficult to know all of the events in the right order, but I know that upon completion of my mission I will begin a retreat to Alaska alone to meditate and rejuvenate my lost energies. Doing this intense work will require that I break all ties with everyone I have a relationship with so I can focus. So it comes to be that in my preparation for leaving, I need to let go of the past.

As I sit on my hospital bed with my legs crossed, facing the window, there is a man's voice coming from just outside my open door. I recognize the voice as belonging to someone who has been some sort of authoritative figure in my life, but I cannot tell who it is. I can also hear the shuffle of several other people in the hallway, and sense that they are all lined up on one side of the door. I do not turn to try to see the man or the others outside of my door. I know why they are there and looking at them would not help the cause. The man starts listing off names of people with whom I have had important relationships. There are a lot of people out there in the hallway, maybe two-hundred or more. They are a mix of relatives, friends, past co-workers, girlfriends, crushes, old roommates, teachers, flight instructors, and just about anyone I might be able to recall as having some significance in my life at one point or another.

The voice first calls out the names of people that I remember from my childhood. Several names of classmates from elementary school are called, friends that I met in kindergarten. As each name is called, the person owning the name walks across the open doorway in the hall and leaves the area. I don't see this happening because I refuse to turn around, but I know it is happening. I can hear them. For most of the people whose names are called, I barely flinch. I remain sitting on my bed facing the window away from the door and keep my eyes closed. This is a final goodbye to all of these people in my life. For some people, I have to fight the urge to turn and say goodbye or to at least catch a glimpse of the person. As the names of childhood friends are being called, one stands out. It is the name of a girl I was secretly in love with in kindergarten. I doubt she ever knew how I felt for her, yet here she is as an adult, walking past my door, silently saying goodbye so that I could move forward. I want to look, but I know I have to stay motionless and breathe deeply as each name is called and as each person walks out of my life for good.

Sensing how serious the situation is, I feel a lot of love coming from the hallway. All of these people are gathered together to say goodbye, so I can get on with my new mission in life. It is bitter sweet. I realize that  most of these people are meeting each other for the first time and that they all now have a common bond and the fact that they were all called together to help me will keep them all together for the rest of their lives. Many of them are crying outside my door as we all know we will never see each other again.

More names are called and more people walk by, all in chronological order of my life. A name stands out. It is the name of one of my elementary school teachers. She told my parents when I was in the first grade that there was something special about me, that I was holy. Again, I want to turn and say goodbye and to thank her for giving my parents a bit of hope, but I do not move. More names are called. The years flash through my mind as the people walk past my door. It feels as though my entire life is walking away from me. I feel a sense of freedom which grows stronger and stronger as each person walks away. I continue to let go of my past and I become a free man, ready to move on with no ties to the past.

*To be continued in Chapter 7...*

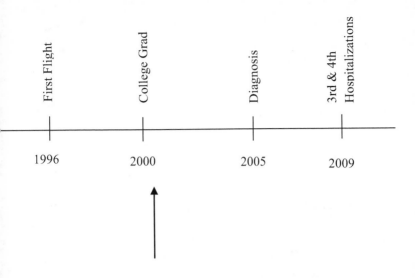

First Flight | College Grad | Diagnosis | 3rd & 4th Hospitalizations

1996      2000      2005      2009

## Chapter 6: Forced Flight and Musical Desires

- Spokane, WA / Fairbanks, AK / Barrow, AK /
Minneapolis, MN / Duluth, MN -
- June 2000 to May 2001 - Age 25 -
-Looking back -

My new job as a flight instructor opened my eyes to a world of endless possibilities. I was stuck in a trance, thinking about how far I had come. It was less than five years prior when the idea of being a pilot was nothing more than a fantasy. It was just a dream, a thought, and at first it was something unattainable. But I made it. And it's not like I just became a private pilot. No, I had become a commercial pilot and flight instructor. My success in landing my first job right out of college was dangerous in a way, because it helped push me towards the idea that I could do anything I put my mind to, that I could follow any dream no matter how huge it might seem, and no matter how it might affect my life.

Working as a flight instructor was fun. The students were great in Spokane. I looked forward to every morning. Every drive to the airport was a promising drive. I never dreaded a single day on the job in Spokane.

I learned a lot about flying from being a flight instructor. My shortcomings as a commercial pilot showed up easily when I began to teach others how to fly. That's the way it works. I had heard people say that the best way to learn something is to teach it, and I came to believe in that.

New relationships sprouted in Spokane just as they had at UND in Grand Forks. Making friends was easy. I was a social person, and I enjoyed going out for dinner and drinks with new people. I never felt alone those days.

I especially did not feel alone after meeting a certain young woman in Spokane. As with many other people, she and I clicked immediately, but as more than just friends. We spent that summer getting to know each other pretty well, but my dreams would split us apart.

Life seemed exciting with my new career. But soon after starting flying in Spokane, something began to change. I didn't notice it at the time, but I became very agitated with my place in life. I loved flying, but I wanted to try flying somewhere new. I wanted something different. I wanted a change.

After just two months in Spokane, a place that had served me well for what my needs were, I felt I must move on. Day two there may as well have been my last, for my eyes set upon Alaska so hard, like I was adjusting the focus of the strongest of telescopes in the direction of the supposed last frontier. I needed any frontier really, any at all would do, for it came to be that I knew not how to rest or to relax. My skin began to crawl. It wasn't the place that made my skin crawl. It was my mind. I didn't understand how it worked. Nor did I know that I *needed* to know how my mind worked. This time in Spokane was the beginning, the beginning of the end of my sanity and stability.

The summer of 2000 would take me north to Alaska, but first I drove west. I packed in the back of my pick-up a tent and sleeping bag and the few things that I camped with, just a couple pots, a lantern, and a clean hunting knife that I never used for hunting. I've never been much of a hunter. I did not need that knife for hunting but maybe for protection from a crazed bear, as if I could have taken on a bear with only a knife. The rest of what I packed was not anything special, except for my guitar. I smoked as I drove, and I drove with open windows to let the wind in and out and to have no feeling of being closed in too tightly, for I just couldn't handle those feelings of being in a box. I was doing what I needed to do without question. It was so easy. I did not allow any resistance from any person be it friend or family. Not even a woman's love could keep me still. The resistance from the responsibility of work was easy to avoid by simply quitting my job. And so, I put in my two-week notice. I would soon no longer be a flight instructor in Spokane.

Alaska was on my mind, but first I drove to Seattle to learn how to take off from and land an airplane on water. Two days of flight training were scheduled with Kenmore Air, a corporate sea-plane charter operation in Seattle, the largest of its kind in the lower 48 states. Since I would be trying to fly in Alaska, I knew my chances of finding work would be better if I had the sea-plane rating added to my commercial pilot certificate. I also scheduled the training because I knew I would love it, that it would be fun and that it was another sort of adventure that I needed to help me breathe and to keep my head on straight. All I ever wanted was something new, something I didn't understand, more than a challenge really and more than a hobby. I needed a way of life that nobody could copy.

Before my scheduled flight training began, I received a call from Kenmore Air saying that the trainer airplane I would be using was down for maintenance unexpectedly and they were sorry, but I would have to reschedule. These were good people and I was not upset with them, understanding that these things happen and if a plane breaks you should fix it while you have it on the ground in one piece before you fly it and realize you left something go just a little too long. So I let my mission pass from my mind and I never rescheduled the training. I headed south from Seattle.

I cannot remember all the places I camped, but I drove south along the west coast, keeping the ocean in view and I was so right to do so because the sight of the ocean made me smile so big on the inside that it actually showed a little even on my face. With the smell of salt and seaweed added, I was stuck in a trance that I feared might end and I began to wish for death in that place so perfect and fresh. I figured to die while feeling so good must be the right way to go, not in tears or sadness, but in joy and excitement and with looking forward to the next big adventure. That's what death was to me, just another adventure, because it seemed to involve so much change and so much of the unknown. I wasn't sure what all the fuss was about really, about death and dying and sadness.

While in Spokane, restlessness became part of my personality. But during that trip south along the west coast, I felt at ease and as if everything was ok although everything was not ok. My adventure was filled with feelings of being ok everywhere I turned. Those days I now recognize as unique and especially important to remember. I stayed alert from early morning without napping at any hour, and remained wide awake into the late evening, late enough to lay on my back and scour the sky for stars, planets, other worlds that I imagined were so close.

My trip took me south along the west coast into the Redwoods where I spent some time camping and hiking. Then I made my way to Lake Tahoe for one night. I left Tahoe to go to Colorado to visit a friend, but I never made it there. Instead, I felt that it was finally time to get back to Spokane to do my final packing for my move to Alaska. It was that silly heart of mine, telling me to turn left. I drove north and eventually met up with the Snake River in Idaho. Even driving in my truck alongside the water, I felt part of the river. I felt like it was guiding me to where I was supposed to be going. I guess I would take anything that made me think I was doing something right. But in reality, I was just wandering through life at the time. I had no patience or ability to commit to work or a relationship. But I was still young and it felt ok to be like that. I continued on and soon found myself in Fairbanks.

Being in Alaska made me feel privy to a great secret. I knew something special that most of the world's population did not even know they were missing. There was peace in Alaska. It was easy to sense that much. I could see new colors in my mind that were set free by the nature and beauty of the land, and thoughts of never going back to the lower 48 took over my senses. Thoughts of letting go of all the people in my life were popping into my mind. I had the realization that Alaska would be the place where I would die, where my body would return to the earth, and where my soul would finally be set free. Alaska felt like my new home, but still I could not rest.

After a few weeks of being in Alaska, I took a job at a small airline based in Fairbanks as a dispatch assistant. It wasn't a pilot position, but all things considered, it would be only a matter of time until I was offered a flying job with the company. It took a few months, but then I was in the air with a move to Barrow on the north coast for my base of operations. It was winter in Alaska and I was flying on very little experience. I had only two months of work as a flight instructor prior to flying in Barrow, and it turned out that I could have used a lot more experience before trying to fly in the Alaska winter weather. I couldn't handle the job. I thought the flight operations were not safe in terms of being expected to break FAA flight regulations in order to complete flights in adverse weather conditions. Expecting to receive an FAA violation if I continued flying with the company, I quit the job without even giving two-week's notice. That was a big mistake. I should have at least given a notice.

I felt like I was making excuses, trying to give myself a reason to leave Alaska. If I had listened to my heart, I may have stayed. Another job could have been found, even if it wasn't a flying job, although I knew I didn't want to do something that I wasn't passionate about. My time in Alaska had been short, only five months. With the end of that flying job came an opportunity to feel open to other dreams.

The music that began to captivate my mind back at

UND in North Dakota started to overtake my senses. I dreamed often of becoming an audio engineer, working with recording equipment, paying close attention to all the subtle details of the sound waves, picking out certain frequencies to amplify or compress or modify with mystical effects processors. The idea of being an audio engineer began to overtake the idea of continuing to fly. I just had to try it, go for it no matter what happened, and having found myself done with Alaska I realized I was free to try something new.

After I quit the flying job in Alaska, I moved in with my parents, back in Fridley, Minnesota, a suburb of Minneapolis. I didn't know what I was going to do. I was stumped. I wanted to fly, but after two flying jobs, I got a sense that flying wasn't the answer. I was unhappy deep inside and I thought that the type of work I did would solve my problems. Music was on my mind. All I wanted to do was write and record music. I set up my recording gear in my parents' basement and for two months I played, wrote, and recorded. During that time I didn't look for work, but instead let my dream of working as an audio engineer in a recording studio grow so large that I finally had to take action. I started researching schools for audio recording degrees. I contacted several engineers at different studios around the country, mostly L.A., Nashville, and New York, to get opinions about the different schools. A college in Winter Park, Florida, next to Orlando, by the name of Full Sail – Real World Education (now Full Sail University) was the clear winner as far as I could tell. I enrolled to begin the Associate Degree program in June 2001. In March, I left my parents' place and moved north back to Duluth, Minnesota where an old college roommate was still living. My plan was to stay there until the end of May, then move to Florida to begin school. Matt, one of my best friends, was renting a house and recently lost his roommate and certainly could use the help with rent.

I found a server job at The Ground Round in Duluth and worked about 20 hours per week while I was waiting to go to Florida. I was drinking on my time off and although I still enjoyed a good party, for those three months in Duluth, I seemed just fine drinking with Matt or even just by myself. I had all of my recording gear set up in the basement of the house and I recall enjoying many drinks alone while writing and recording songs. I didn't think about the alcohol one way or another. It was just part of who I was. I had started drinking seven years prior when I first got to college and just never stopped to think about the drinking, what it was doing to me, or why I continued. And I drank to get drunk. I was never one to go out for a social drink and limit myself to one or two. If I had one, then I wanted to get drunk.

Duluth was an easy place to live for a few months while I waited for school to start. That was where I started college, so it felt comfortable. I waited patiently to move to Florida.

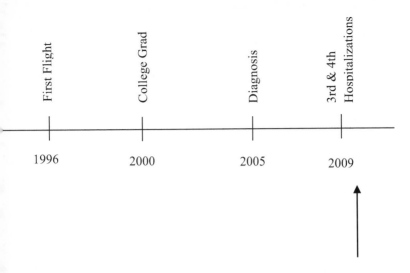

## Chapter 7:  Fairview – The Show

- Minneapolis, MN - June 9th, 2009 - Age 34 -

*- In the moment -*

***Continued from Chapter 5:***  *I continue to let go of my past and I become a free man, ready to move on with no ties to the past.*

The difference between the present and the future is becoming increasingly difficult to decipher.  The past is easy to see and easy to understand, as it has all led to what is happening now.  I am having a problem with understanding what is happening outside of the hospital.  At any given moment, I follow one of two trains of thought.  The first is that when I first came into Fairview, I saw the future.  I saw the

67

worst of all wars. I saw people close to me die. Then I saw world peace. Because seeing those things scared me, I tried to go back in time in order to prevent the wars from happening. I went back in time, but in the process of going back in time, I became God. But I was God in human form, which means that I became Jesus, and that means that Jesus had returned and he had used my body in order to do so.

It makes sense that Jesus would use someone like me to show himself. Of course he would use someone like me who has already died once on the inside. I reason that my mental illness has played a major role in allowing this transformation to occur and that if Jesus chose a person with mental illness, then mental illness must not really be an illness at all. Rather, it is a state of mind, a state of ultimate awareness that allows communication through dimensions that most people cannot detect, comprehend, or understand. Because people cannot understand this state of awareness, it makes sense that the people who do not have these gifts would use a label such as "illness." I understand why I have been chosen to save the world. It is obvious that the world needs saving, even if it means saving one person at a time. But I am sure that I can save more than one person at a time.

The media has recently been covering many stories of suicides within the military. There seems to be a great deal of stigma in our armed forces around mental illness. I figure if I can kill the stigma, then I can stop the suicides. Since Jesus chose me, a person with mental illness, people will no longer be afraid of mental illness. Our soldiers who need help will not be afraid of asking for help. And those around them will not be afraid to offer help. The military's suicides will stop. Then the trend will spread. Soon there will be no mental illness stigma anywhere in the world. But there will still be problems.

Although mental illness has its positive side, there can be a negative side as well. I have come to believe that the evil people in the world, such as Osama Bin Laden, are mentally ill. But unlike me, these evil people have run in the wrong direction with their illness. They too have a gift of communication through other dimensions, but I figure that they are communicating with the devil, Satan himself. And it seems that if the world can understand mental illness, then all wars will end and there will be world peace. It's simple.

All of this is part of the confusion in my head here in Fairview Hospital. I'm trying to determine if my hallucinations were a vision of the future or a vision of things that actually happened. To continue with the path of seeing the future, it seems I have a holy war on my hands. Based on witnessing the future, I have the knowledge of what needs to happen to end the wars. That viewpoint, the viewpoint that says "I know the future and I am part of making that future happen" is the cause of my thinking that I will soon be out of the hospital and going on a mission with President Obama.

But there is another train of thought that I find myself flipping to. It is a train of thought that is much more relaxing, calming and peaceful. It is a train of thought that causes me to want to celebrate.

As opposed to thinking that my hallucinations were visions of the future, I find myself also thinking that they were visions of what has been happening in real-time. So now, while I am in Fairview, the mightiest war in history just happened and is over. World peace is here. Worldwide awareness of mental illness has been achieved. There will be no more suicides. There will be no more stigma surrounding mental illness. All of this has happened because Jesus showed himself through me. The world has witnessed the return of Jesus. Now it is time to celebrate. Now it is time to party, and it's going to be a big party. I realize the celebration that I feel within me is felt around the world. There is a party being planned right now, and I will be the guest of honor.

I realize that I am no longer Jesus. He has shown himself through me and disappeared just as quickly as he showed up. But I will be celebrated as the vessel who allowed the world to be saved. Many things are happening at once. There is a documentary film being made about me. In fact, I am being filmed right now as I am in the hospital. Every security camera that I can see, along with others that I have yet to discover, are focused on me and lead to a studio where the movie directors and producers are. I know some of the people who are directing and producing the film. One of them is Michael, the owner of a recording studio that I worked in while living in Portland, Oregon, in 2003/2004. He is in charge of the audio production for the documentary. He has placed microphones on almost all of the patients and staff members in the hospital. Everything I say is being recorded. Every breath in and out of my mouth can be picked up by these microphones. I like that Michael is involved in the film. I understand now why my life took me to Portland and to work for Michael. In the studio where Michael is recording me, there is another Michael. Michael Moore.

I understand that Michael Moore has been working his entire life to become the greatest documentary film director in the world, and that all of his work has led to this opportunity, to create the documentary about the coming of world peace. He has been put on this Earth in order to capture the story of the return of Jesus and the destruction of mental illness stigma everywhere. It has become Michael Moore's job to tell the story of how all war has ended and how it came to be that one unlikely man, such as me, was able to allow the power of God to work through him to save the world. But Michael and Michael are not alone. There is another Michael with them who prefers to go by Mike.

Mike is a friend, a guy I worked with for a couple years delivering furniture at the time of my diagnosis. He is interested in film and I have known that he will end up sometime in his lifetime as a great film director. His time has come now. It has worked out perfectly for Mike, this opportunity of a lifetime. I know that Michael Moore has a team of people who started researching my life, looking for people I know, looking for friends, family, co-workers, neighbors, everyone you can imagine. And of course having worked with Mike, the connection has been established between Mike and Michael Moore. Michael Moore enlisted Mike as his assistant director. Now Mike is on the map in a huge way. And they are getting along as if they have been working together their entire lives. It was meant to be, the three Michaels in the recording studio.

It's a unique setup, the studio. These guys are not making a traditional movie. There is no rehearsal, no script, no "action" being called. All cameras are running, many cameras, and all microphones are live capturing everything I say. I realize that the studio is where the documentary is being produced. It's in the new Twins stadium which I know wasn't even finished being built when I came into the hospital, but it must be finished now, because I am getting visions of what is happening there in the stadium. It's the first event to be held in the new stadium and it is more than sold out. People from all over the world are lined up waiting to get inside.

The studio where Mike and the two Michaels are working is somewhere in the stadium and they are recording me live and displaying the action directly to the big screen in the stadium. The stadium is filled with people watching the live documentary of me, the person who helped stop the wars and saved the world. All my old friends are there, all of them. I have lost a lot of friends over the recent years because of my bipolar disorder, but now everyone understands me, understands why I have been chosen to have this disorder, and they have all come back to me to help me celebrate. My friends and family are in the center of the stadium. There is a huge stage and the band Phish is playing some of my old favorites, while many other bands are there waiting to play. Everyone is grooving to Phish. Everyone is dancing. Everyone is watching the big screen, watching me as I am in the hospital dealing with calming down my mania. But they are watching more than what is happening to me in the present moment. They are also seeing my old home videos being played on the big screen.

I realize that Michael Moore really did his research. Apparently he went to my home and took all of my home videos from my small fire-proof safes. Everywhere I went over the years, all of my moves around the country, I often had a video camera capturing something that seemed most likely useless. But now Michael Moore has all of these tapes and he is mixing them into the live documentary. The people in the Twins Stadium are seeing videos of me as a child, me in my junior high years, high school, college, and on and on, leading up to the present moment. It's quite a show, and that's what it comes to be called in my head… "The Show."

Now I know that as part of "The Show," most, if not all of the patients around me are not really patients. There are a few guys who are in a famous band together, but I don't really know their band. I just know that they will be going to the stadium soon to play in "The Show." Right now though, they are being displayed on the big screen just as I am because they are interacting with me in the hospital. It's sort of like an enormous joke is being played on me. But I have figured out the joke. Everyone is trying to watch me. At first, they don't think I know, but I do. And I try to play along, acting as if I don't know I am being filmed, but I can't last long with that. I give in and start talking to the camera and say things to the different people in the hospital who have microphones on their bodies. I let everyone in the studio know that I know they are watching me. Now we are all having fun together. Soon I will be brought to the stadium and I will be honored there.

Evening is approaching, still Wednesday, day two in Fairview. I want to go to the stadium. But I realize that the live documentary that is being made of me is not going to be just a two hour movie. I realize that I probably won't get out of the hospital anytime soon. This documentary will continue for my entire hospital stay. Everyone in the stadium will watch my recovery in the hospital, to see how it's done, to see how a champion recovers from a manic episode. But it's more than just the people in the stadium. Now "The Show" is being broadcast all over the world. People everywhere will watch me in the hospital for however long it takes me to recover. I understand that this could be a long show and decide to go to bed. I slide under my bed covers and feel very happy, very content. I can be patient and wait for a full recovery before going to the stadium to join the celebration. I fall asleep easily.

*To be continued in Chapter 9…*

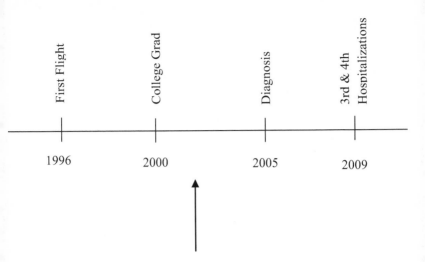

First Flight

College Grad

Diagnosis

3rd & 4th Hospitalizations

1996            2000            2005            2009

**Chapter 8:  Noticing God, But Still No Answers**

- Orlando, FL - 2001, 2002 - Ages 26, 27 -

- Looking back -

May finally rolled around and it was time to go to Florida. I had contacted the music recording school and they set me up with a roommate. He seemed like a cool guy and actually turned out to be one of the most interesting people I have ever met. I was uncomfortable with how much pot he smoked. It seemed he couldn't get through a single morning without getting high. So, there was a drug issue there with this particular roommate. I had smoked marijuana before, just a couple times when I was about 20 during my second year at college in Duluth. That was before I started flying. Once I started flying, I became fairly paranoid about even being around someone who was smoking pot, fearing that I might take in the second-hand smoke and fail a drug test. So, although I was in Florida for audio recording school and not flying at the time, I simply did not want to jeopardize my pilot's license. But I soon found myself weak and occasionally enjoying marijuana.

Being a student at Full Sail was mentally demanding more from a physiological viewpoint versus an academic point of view. The classes were fairly easy for me. For the most part, the learning could be done by intense memorization. It was all about the use of the technical recording gear and not so much about any sort of philosophy or rhetoric and therefore didn't require much thinking or debating, in my opinion. The recording program was an associate of science degree and consisted of two years' worth of classes crammed into one year, with classes being held 24 hours a day. My typical schedule was class from 9 AM to 1 PM, then 5 PM to 9 PM, then again from 1 AM to 5 AM. There was no room for good rest. I didn't think much of it at the time since it was the same for all the students, but I now know that the schedule was horrible for my health. Mountain Dew was my main course throughout any given day, as well as cigarettes. This was a dangerous year for me, pushing me closer to instability.

The first three months of the recording program were far too easy for me. Classes were typically one month long, with a few lasting two months. I was highly disappointed in the program, lacking the challenge I had expected. I had heard from many students who were further along in the program that things got a lot tougher starting in the fourth month, but I was impatient. At this point it was August of 2001. I felt like I was wasting my time and money and I decided to pursue flying again, after only three months into the program. I checked out the hiring situation with some of the airlines that had good connections with the aviation program at The University of North Dakota and learned that Piedmont Airlines (US Airways Express) would be conducting interviews during the first week of October 2001. I applied for the job and got accepted for an interview. Then I took a two-month leave of absence from school, remaining as an enrolled student, just in case I wanted to come back. I decided that it would be best to show up to the Piedmont Airlines interview with a current flying job of any sort, so I went to Daytona for training to be a banner-tow pilot, flying banners along the beaches of the east coast.

Soon after beginning the banner-tow training came September 11th and all flying stopped. Initially, the interview with Piedmont was up in the air. I waited almost a month in Daytona to resume banner-tow training which was, along with sight-seeing flights, the last type of flying operations the FAA allowed to resume after 9-11. Eventually, the Piedmont Airlines interview was cancelled. I decided I would continue with the audio recording program at Full Sail, which would start up again for me in November. I had a few weeks to kill, so I went to Minneapolis to hang out with my family before returning to school.

Having taken two months off from school, upon returning I was placed in an entirely different class of students. The degree program started each month as opposed to consisting of quarters or semesters. On day one of my return to school, I sat front row and center in my first class. Surrounding me were three guys who obviously knew each other fairly well. They were joking around and having fun. One guy was especially loud. We introduced ourselves to each other. The loud guy was Blake and the other two were Pat and Peter. There was something unique about these guys although I couldn't tell what it was. I could tell right away that they were good guys.

Soon after returning to classes, I learned that Blake, Pat, and Peter were the worship band members at a local non-denominational Christian church, East Pointe. I don't recall the conversation that led to this, but they invited me to play with them in the worship band. I also don't recall exactly how I felt at the time about going to church, much less playing in the worship band. I was about 26 years old and it was the first time since high school that I had even gone to church. I think in general I was starting to acknowledge the fact that I was feeling lost in my life. I felt a void and I was trying to fill it with something. Going to East Pointe felt good. The atmosphere was relaxed with a small congregation. There was always coffee and doughnuts and it was fun playing in the worship band. But I felt a little out of place, at times feeling almost like a fraud. I wasn't sure that I belonged in the worship band because I wasn't sure what I believed about God and religion in general. I had thoughts about believing in some sort of God, but did I believe in Jesus? Did I believe in the Bible? Was I a Christian? It was the beginning of examining those questions and it was uncomfortable.

Blake, Pat, Peter, and I spent a lot of time together outside of classes. They had been holding a Bible study and I joined the group. Again, it was fairly uncomfortable for me. Those three guys were solid in their religious beliefs and I was far from that.

I was working hard at school and having fun with Blake, Pat, and Peter. For a while, Pat and I played racquet ball on our time off from classes. I wasn't drinking much anymore. Part of it was that with the busy school schedule, there wasn't much free time to drink. And another part was that Blake, Pat, and Peter were influencing me with their lack of drinking. Also, the more I felt a part of the church, the less it seemed I drank. But it wasn't something I was conscious of. My drinking habits just slowly changed, but it would later prove to not be a permanent change.

During my time in Florida, my life got a little strange in terms of my faith and religion. As I became more involved with church, I began experiencing something new. I didn't see it coming, and it certainly caught me off-guard. There must have been a specific day, some defined moment where I would have had the realization, but I cannot remember

81

anything of the sort. It just happened that I found myself getting close to God. And that's when the trouble began. That's when Satan started messing with my life. Before living in Florida, I had never experienced anything close to evil. But as soon as I started getting close to God, evil swooped in to push me away.

On what seemed to be a peaceful night, my friend Pat and I were standing in the parking lot of Peter's apartment complex, me leaning on the side of Pat's truck bed having a smoke, Pat standing a few feet away also smoking. We weren't talking about anything special, probably something over-rated such as which manufacture made the best vocal microphone for the money. We were just there, smoking, talking, as we enjoyed the warm Orlando nighttime air, nothing more than two guys in their mid to late twenties, hanging out, doing nothing. Everything was normal. Then out of nowhere Pat looked like he was going to puke. I asked if he was ok, and he said no, that he felt really weird. This came on quickly. From the time he started looking sick to him answering my question was about 12 seconds. Then about two seconds after that I felt the worst feeling of my entire life. This was a feeling I pray I never feel again and pray that no person will have to ever feel. It was evil, pure evil. It took about one second for evil to pass through me. My nervous system overloaded with stimulation and all I knew for that second was dread and death. When I say that I felt it, I don't mean that it was a feeling like happiness or sadness. I felt it in the physical sense. It had to be the devil. It had to be the devil that passed through Pat making him feel sick. It had to be the devil that passed through me making me feel dread and death. And seven seconds after I felt the evil, I figure it had to be the devil who showed himself through the young man fifty feet away from Pat and me in the parking lot firing a pistol, the smoking barrel caught by Pat's eyesight, the breaking of the sound barrier witnessed by our ears, the shock of which caused me to duck, then realize Pat had started running away, so I followed.

Although there were those serious moments in Florida, I still had a lot of fun and experienced a light-hearted and carefree atmosphere. It wasn't all about God and Satan.

There was a continuous bit of humor than hung around Blake, Pat, Peter, and me. It revolved around a song that was at some point played on a radio show, The Bob and Tom Show in Chicago. Maybe you have heard it. It is called "The Toast Song," by Heywood Banks. A performance of the song can be easily found by a search on google.com or youtube.com. I think it was Pat who introduced the song to the rest of us. The fact that this song had meaning to me will probably not make sense to you at this point in my story, but I will come back to it later and explain. For now, just know that "The Toast Song" was, for my friends and me in Florida, a sort of inside joke with a lot of personal meaning behind it. The song was one that we would occasionally sing. It was something simple that made us laugh. Four years later, "The

Toast Song" would become part of my understanding of the universe during my first major manic episode.

The end of my studies at Full Sail approached quickly. I became very unsure about pursuing work as an audio engineer. After putting some serious thought to it, I decided that I should be flying again, and that I could work on music in my free time as a hobby. I interviewed for a flight instructor job in Orlando that was set up through a connection I had at church, but once again, I started faltering on my decision to fly. Soon, I found myself researching opportunities at different recording studios, one of which was in Minneapolis. I cannot recall my feelings about wanting to move to Minneapolis. I must have missed my family, and perhaps some friends, although most of my friends from college were by that time scattered around the country. Finally I decided to leave Florida. I was on the road, only a couple hours into Georgia when I received a phone call from the chief flight instructor where I had interviewed for the flight instructor job in Orlando. I let the call go to voicemail. Then I checked the message. I was offered the job, but I never even returned the call, not even to let the guy know that I was leaving and would not be taking the job.

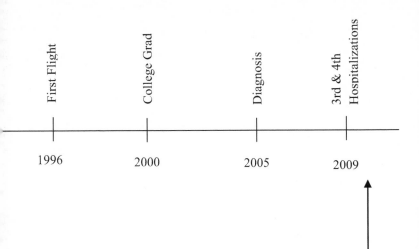

First Flight

College Grad

Diagnosis

3rd & 4th Hospitalizations

|———————|————————|—————————|—————————|————————

1996            2000            2005            2009

**Chapter 9:  Present Yourself Well**

- Minneapolis, MN - June 2009 - Age 34 -

- *In the moment* -

*Continued from chapter 7:  I can be patient and wait for a full recovery before going to the stadium to join the celebration.  I fall asleep easily.*

I open my eyes from a night of heavy sleep. Everything is different.  As soon as I wake, I realize that all of my thoughts about "The Show" have come to me from the future, that none of it has happened yet.  My visions of the wars ending and visions of world peace have come from the future.  The three Michaels are not in a recording studio together.  They don't even know each other.  There is not a documentary film being made about me.  There is no celebration. The Twins stadium is not filled with people. I need to leave the hospital so I can take care of my mission so that the future events will come to be. I need to get out now. I need to see the President. I need to escape.

There is a long hallway with two sets of double doors at each end. I focus on one end of the hallway. There is something on the wall next to the doors about the size of a light switch cover with two small lights on it, one red, and one green. I watch for my signal. All I need is a green light telling me to "go." But I realize that standing next to the door is not a good idea. The staff will see me loitering and tell me to move. They will know I am trying to escape. If they only knew why I had to go, they would open the doors wide for me, but they don't get it. And I can't tell them. It's not their fault and I don't blame them.

I have a vague memory of someone being in my room last night, sometime in the middle of the night, trying to give me medication. It's a hazy memory. It feels like they were trying to give me the wrong medication and all I can remember is trying to calmly tell them that either the medication wasn't the right one, or that it wasn't the right time for my medication. This person, I can barely picture their face, kept trying to get me to take the drugs, but I refused. This is a good thing. I know that this person eventually gave in and let me go back to sleep without the meds, so that must mean that the hospital staff is beginning to understand that I don't need medication. That's certainly what I have come to believe, that I don't need the meds.

But my psychiatrist is still having the nurses bring medication to me. I figure he knows that I don't need the medication, but that he must follow the rules and give me meds. I can tell that he knows I will stop taking the meds as soon as I am out of the hospital. They just aren't for me anymore. I think about how I wanted to voluntarily be admitted to the hospital for new medication, and now that I have it, I don't want it. I guess the meds worked. They must have, because I feel OK. And if I'm feeling OK, then I don't need the meds.

The last couple of days go by slowly. I still feel pretty special, like I know I have been put on Earth for a specific purpose, but I don't tell anyone that I am feeling this. I just want to go home, sleep in my own bed next to my wife. I'm sick of the visits here. I want to go home. And that is what soon happens. After all the paper work is completed, the last words from my psychiatrist to me are "present yourself well."

I take his words very seriously, because deep inside my heart I can feel the truth that says I shouldn't leave the hospital yet. I am not stable. I know that much for sure, but I want out of here. I will not tell anyone that I am still receiving messages from God, although they have minimized. Nor will I tell anyone about all of the synchronicities that are taking place everywhere I look. The secrets of how to stop the wars are still in my mind, so I will have to keep quiet about that as well. I will have to do as the doctor ordered. I will have to present myself well.

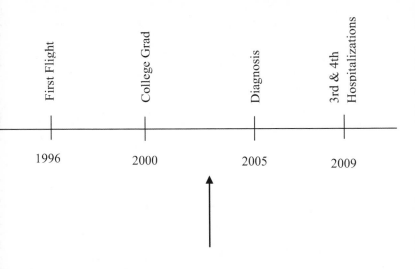

## Chapter 10: Bouncing Around

- Aberdeen, SD / Portland, OR / Duluth, MN / Vancouver,
WA / Minneapolis, MN -

- Sept. 2002 to July 2005 - Ages to 27 to 30 -

- Looking back -


My time in Aberdeen, Portland, and Duluth, was all about following my passions. I was gaining experience toward dreams that didn't have a true destination. I was focused on my work, but not focused enough to stay in one place for very long. Also I was not focused enough to choose one path, one career. The battle between flying and music continued.

After leaving Florida, I moved to Aberdeen, South Dakota for a flight instructor job. I spent all my free time writing and recording music by myself. I lasted nine months on the job, then felt the need to move to Portland where my friend Josh from college was living. I thought for sure that we would start a band.

After one month of exploring the northwest, I decided to look for work as an audio engineer in Portland. I went to all of the studios in town looking for an intern position, and finally found a guy who took me on as an unpaid intern for two months. At the end of the two months, I was hired full time and stayed on for a total of one year. It was the longest I had lasted on a job so far.

In the spring of 2004 I met Shannon, a girlfriend that would prove to be part of my initial treatment for my broken mind. She lived in Vancouver, Washington, just next door to Portland. About three months after we met I began to worry heavily about money and decided the best thing to do was to get back into flying which would eventually lead to a decent paying job at a major airline. So after one year of working at the recording studio, I looked for flying jobs and found one in Duluth, Minnesota. Shannon stayed in Vancouver and we thought we could put up with the long distance for a while until I might be able to find a flying job back in the northwest.

I lasted only about seven months in Duluth as a flight instructor, training Cirrus Design customers in their new airplanes. I thought I needed to be with Shannon in Vancouver. I thought that being with her would fix my problems, take all my pain away. I didn't know how much pain I had inside me, so much that it was impossible for one person to make better. But I quit my flying job in Duluth and moved back west. Shannon and I rented a house together in Vancouver and I looked for work.

I expected to be happy when I moved back west to be with Shannon. But I wasn't. I fell into a deep depression, hitting rock bottom out of nowhere. It was like I was crippled. I couldn't sleep, couldn't get out of bed, couldn't get myself going for the day, and couldn't do anything except cry. All I knew is that I wanted to die.

When I left my flying job in Duluth to be with my Shannon in Vancouver, WA, I took the first job that I could find, a terrible sales job, selling windows to home owners. It didn't matter that it wasn't flying because I figured I would find another flying job in a while. So for the time being, I would work the sales jobs. But it was all a big scam. The company I worked for had their sales people approach home owners with the idea that the home owner was receiving a free home energy audit. The situation always turned into pressuring the home owners to buy new windows to make their home more energy efficient. I couldn't stand the sales tactics. I wasn't any good at sales. If a person told me "no," that they didn't want windows, that was fine with me. But according to management, I was supposed to battle all the "no's" and fight for a "yes" at all costs. I couldn't do it. Especially after the home owner thought I was entering their home for nothing more than a free energy audit.

I was on my way to a sales appointment when I started bawling while driving. I had to pull over, and stopped at a gas station. That's when I called Shannon and asked for the number of her old therapist. At the time, Shannon was the only person in my life I knew of who had been to a therapist. I didn't know where else to start. I called that therapist and told her that I was messed up, that I was depressed and confused and scared and that all I did was cry and feel hopeless. That therapist gave me the number of another therapist and the process began.

I can recall the first meeting with my therapist. He was a young guy, about my age actually, or maybe just a bit older. That fact alone made me uncomfortable. He had just completed his Ph.D. and was just starting out in the field. I was one of his first guinea pigs. That added to my discomfort with him. He was too careful with me. I am a person who likes abrupt advice, but this guy seemed afraid of saying the wrong thing. It was obviously not a perfect fit, but as far as I knew at the time, my discomfort could have been just from the concept of visiting a therapist at all, since it was my first time doing so. After about six weeks, he thought I should try antidepressants, so he referred me to a psychiatrist who could prescribe the medication. We continued our visits however. In the meantime, I had quit the sales job.

On my first visit with the psychiatrist, she gave me free samples of an antidepressant. I was out of work at the time, and she thought she was helping by giving me the free samples. Looking back, it's how quickly and easily she offered me the medication that surprises me. We didn't talk about my drinking, how I should stop that. We didn't talk about nutrition. We didn't talk about meditation or relaxation techniques. We didn't talk about exercise. We didn't talk about much at all, just that I was depressed.

One thing that we did talk about though, was the fact that if I were to accept her offer of antidepressants, I would not be able to fly while being treated with medication. My depression at this point could be considered "situational," potentially stemming from making too many quick decisions about jobs and moving around the country and maybe the build-up of stress associated with my general lack of commitment with work and relationships. I would not be able to fly while taking the medication, but it didn't mean that my flying career was over. At the time, it just meant that I would probably be on the antidepressants for four to six months, and then I could go off the medication and look for another pilot job. I was ok with that idea because I had already experienced periods of no flying and I was always able to get back in the cockpit when the time was right. So, I really didn't think that it was a big deal. I knew how messed up I was and I thought if the antidepressants might help me, it was worth a shot.

The hard part for me was that there wasn't anything major that had happened to me to make me feel this way. I had experienced struggles, but never anything real big like a death of a loved one or a job being taken from me. I was never abused. I had a family who loved me, even if I didn't feel close to them all the time. And I had always had a lot of friends and several girlfriends in my adult life and felt connected to people in general. For me to feel depressed was confusing. I didn't understand where it came from. It seemed illogical. I mentioned the situational factors, the moving around the country and the lack of commitment, all of which could lead to a stressful and potentially depressed situation, but those ideas didn't really seem to add up to enough for me to want to die. But that is what I felt.

June crept up around the corner without me even realizing it was summer. I was too depressed to enjoy much of anything outdoors. I was still seeing the young therapist, but things were not getting better. I called my parents and told them that I was having a hard time. They thought I should move home. I talked to my brother, and he thought I should come home. I talked to both of my sisters, and they thought I should come home. My girlfriend Shannon hated to say it, but she admitted that she also thought I should leave Vancouver, WA and move home to Minneapolis. And I thought the same thing, so I packed my few belongings and said goodbye to Shannon and her family and to a few friends in Portland.

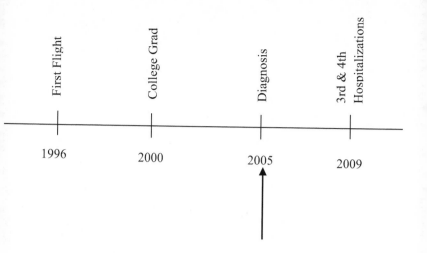

## Chapter 11:  Diagnosis – A Little Too Happy

- Minneapolis, MN – July to September 2005 - Age 30 -

- Looking back -

When I moved home, I literally moved home…to my parents' house.  There wasn't much of a debate in my mind about whether or not it was the right thing to do.  It seemed like the only thing to do, so I did it.  I was already feeling better, having made the decision to come home to my family.  I had less to worry about being at home.  The worry about finding a job was there, but it wasn't as much of a burden as it was in Vancouver while living with Shannon.  I thought a little bit about looking for work, but I really didn't pursue anything for the first six weeks after moving home.  I focused my energy elsewhere.

Ever since I bought my first piece of music recording equipment during flight school, I have had some sort of recording space or home studio wherever I have lived. My first setup was crammed into the corner of my bedroom in an apartment in Grand Forks, ND. I had just a keyboard, a four-track recorder, a microphone with a stand, and my acoustic guitar. Then I bought an electric guitar, an effects-processor and a CD burner so I could record my song mixes to CD from my four-track recorder. After I moved to Spokane, I bought a mandolin. In Spokane, my music gear was also setup in the bedroom of my apartment. Then when I moved to Fairbanks, the gear was setup in the bedroom of a house I was living in. I bought a 12-string guitar while I was in Alaska. During the short time between living in Alaska and moving to Florida for the music recording school, I stayed at my parents' house for a few weeks. I bought another acoustic guitar and an eight-track recorder at that time and had my gear setup in their basement.

Then, as I still waited for school to start in Florida, I moved to Duluth, Minnesota, and lived in a friend's house. I set up all my gear in the basement, but this time I had a small room all to myself, just for my gear. I lined the walls with carpet for acoustic reasons. To me, it was a real studio. I spent a lot of time in that room. When I moved to Florida, I bought a new keyboard, some new microphones, new monitors, a preamp for the microphone, a compressor, and several mouth harps. I also bought a new computer and started recording onto the computer instead of onto the eight-track recorder. I had everything setup once again in my bedroom in a house I was renting. Then I moved to Aberdeen, SD, and bought a bass guitar. I had everything setup in the living room of my apartment this time, rather than in the bedroom.

At this point I did something different. I built a vocal booth in my living room. I made it with 2-by-4's and plywood. I sealed all the seams and corners with expanding liquid foam and lined the inside with carpet. It made for a very acoustically "dead" space with practically no reflections bouncing off the walls of the vocal booth.

When I left Aberdeen and moved to Portland, I setup all my gear in the basement of the house I was living in. The basement was unfinished and very "live" with a lot of echoes. I put up a few walls at odd angles to help prevent the acoustic reflections from building up and added some carpet to the walls. I bought a drum set. My friend Josh had a couple guitars, a banjo, and an accordion. We had a pretty good studio setup. Then I moved to Duluth and rented part of a cabin. I had all the gear setup in the living room. Then I moved to Vancouver and had everything setup in a separate room of a house.

When I left Vancouver and came home to Minneapolis, I setup all my gear in an empty room in the basement of my parents' house. I had everything setup. Then I took it all down because I decided to build a vocal booth in the room and move all my recording equipment into an adjacent room. Unlike the vocal booth that I built in the my apartment in Aberdeen, SD, which was only four feet by four feet in size, this vocal booth would be the real thing, filling up the entire room. I made plans, drew blueprints, and had all the details worked out. I knew what a real vocal booth was meant to do. It's all about keeping any noise, other than the voice you are recording, away from the microphone.

I had no idea that I was getting a little too excited about setting up my recording equipment. I just loved to set up new scenarios with the equipment and that's all it was to me. But it became way too involved. I even insulated the walls to help keep noise transfer to a minimum. But I never finished the project. Something else got in the way. It was the same thing that was helping me to build the vocal booth in the first place, something called mania.

It started slowly. The antidepressants that I started taking in Vancouver began to lift my mood. The problem was that I was a person that needed another drug at the same time to prevent my mood from getting too high. But I didn't know that at the time.

My mind started to put together connections that were just coincidences, giving them more meaning, transforming these events into synchronicities. There was one synchronicity in particular that stood out from the others. In fact, it changed the way I viewed the world and changed my faith in God.

A couple weeks after moving home, I was aimlessly shopping one day at a used CD store. I saw a CD with the word "Toast" in large print on the front of the CD. I immediately picked it up and knew I would buy it. I only saw the front of the CD case. I never even bothered to look at the back of the CD or to determine if "Toast" was the name of the band or an album name. I grabbed it only because of the running joke about the song called "The Toast Song" between Blake, Pat, Peter and me while in Florida in 2001 and 2002. I took the CD home along with a few others that I purchased and tossed them somewhere aimlessly in my bedroom. Then, I forgot all about the CD, as if I had never purchased it. It was about this time that I needed to start thinking about finding a job.

About six weeks after moving into my parents' house, a relative told me about a job opening with a local furniture company. The job was delivering furniture. It was certainly far from flying, but it would do for the time being. At this point, I still had it in my mind that I would be back to flying as soon as my mood stabilized and as soon as I stopped taking the antidepressants. That is not how things would turn out though.

I applied for the job and was hired. I was more than pleased with the company, as they seemed to be a step ahead of any other place I had worked in terms of caring about their employees. There was an obvious focus on health and wellness within the company, and it was apparent that management really wanted everyone to be happy and to find their right place within the company. I felt a little lucky actually, like I had found something good. It felt like more than just a furniture delivery position.

About two weeks into my new job, I was very manic. I wasn't sleeping much at all, but I had a tremendous amount of energy. Life seemed perfect, like everything was in its right place. Looking back, I see that I was extremely happy about delivering furniture, and not concerned at all that I wasn't flying. The euphoria that I was experiencing made every part of my life seem great. I was feeling very social, more social than usual, and I had a hard time being by myself. I had so much energy and so much on my mind that I wanted to be with friends and share with them my excitement for life. I remember saying to my mother one morning as I was leaving for work, "Each day keeps getting better than the one before."

One night I was up late at a friend's place, sitting outside alone on the back deck of his townhouse with my laptop around 2 in the morning. I was writing. On top of my building mania, I smoked a little marijuana which added to my wonderful feelings about the world around me. I had a bunch of CDs with me and I was playing different CDs from my laptop into my headphones. I looked up at the stars. It was a clear night and I felt like I could see everything in the universe. Suddenly, I felt God's presence and felt the entire universe snap into place. There was nothing but peace inside of me and all around me. I was completely euphoric.

While sitting in the manic and high state of awe, I shuffled through my CDs and I saw the "Toast" CD that I had purchased two weeks earlier, but had not yet listened to. I put the CD in my laptop and the first song that played was all about knowing and believing in God. It was the perfect soundtrack to what I was feeling and experiencing at the moment.

Connections fired in my mind about events that had come together over the years to become something of meaning. It all was proving to be about God. These are the thoughts that my mind was referencing as I was listening to the "Toast" CD in the middle of the night. A couple of these items have not been mentioned in earlier chapters. My euphoric thoughts in order...

1. While in Florida in 2001 and 2002, I met Blake, Pat, and Peter.
2. They invited me to join their church and the worship band.
3. There was a running joke about a song that I thought was titled "The Toast Song."
4. While living in Florida, I started to feel like I was close to understanding God and started to feel comfortable with going to church.
5. Strange events happened that made me believe Satan was trying to keep me away from God. I drifted away from my ideas of getting close to God.

6.  I moved from Florida to Aberdeen, South Dakota in September 2002. I started going to a church there. A woman spoke in tongues and it freaked me out. I stopped going to church. I thought I would never go again.

7.  I moved to Portland in June of 2003. I believed that an angel came to me in the night and told me that my son's name would be Avery. But I still thought I would never go to church again. I wasn't sure if I believed in God.

So there I was, manic, euphoric, looking up at the stars, feeling like I understood the universe and that I knew God. And I was listening to that song on the "Toast" CD, and it was all about knowing God. To me, the timing of playing that CD, on top of how I found it and why I bought it, was all much more than a coincidence. In my mania, I believed that everything in this list was clearly all part of God's divine plan, and it was in that moment of playing the "Toast" CD that I witnessed part of that plan for the first time. I believed that it was all a strong and obvious message for me to stop avoiding God and to stop being afraid of Satan. To me, it was proof that God existed.

The question surfaces about whether or not all of that was just coincidence. I wonder how likely it even was that the CD was in that store at the time, being a used CD. There was only one copy, and I just happened to stumble upon it.

Looking at this situation from a stable viewpoint, far from manic, I can easily admit that while I was extremely manic, I may have interpreted just about any CD and any song as highly relevant to what I was experiencing at the time. But even so, I am still at least slightly irked at how closely the song from the "Toast" CD matched my thoughts just moments before I played the song. That's just one example of how I have allowed a web of connections to run in my mind to the point of developing some elaborate plan in the mix of it all.

The night of my epiphany about knowing God and understanding the universe, I slept for fewer than two hours. The day after the "Toast" encounter I was on top of the world. Despite my lack of sleep, work was easy as I was full of energy. Everything around me made sense. I worked that day, delivering furniture. I felt strong, happy, and proud to be doing a good job delivering furniture. After a full day's work, I went home, but I couldn't sit still. In my excitement of what had happened with the "Toast" CD, I called Blake, Pat, and Peter and tried to explain that something amazing had happened. I'm pretty sure they immediately thought something big was wrong with me. I doubt that I made any sense to them as I tried to connect the dots that I had put together, but were so likely to stay far apart from their vantage points. I realized that they weren't getting it, but I didn't care. I felt like something huge had happened and that the universe was in complete alignment. Deep inside, I knew that someday, even if it were a long way away, they would understand what I was talking about. I knew that much for sure. Even if it would take years, I knew they would get it someday. Still restless, I called several other people, and ended up meeting my friend Ali for dinner.

She knew something was wrong with me as soon as we met at the restaurant. I didn't know it at the time, but I was talking fast, having racing thoughts, experiencing flight of ideas, and just not looking like myself. Ali and I met the same time I met Kia, in the fall of 1993. Those two, along with another friend, Sarah, were all roommates at UMD. Ali was so concerned about me that she called Kia and Sarah when I was in the bathroom at the restaurant. Kia and Sarah showed up, and Kia told me I needed to go to the hospital. She didn't have to say it twice. I trusted her, and so I went. I was so manic and euphoric, that I was even excited to be going to the hospital. It felt like a new adventure.

It was the beginning of a long hard look at my entire life, my behavior, moods, decisions, relationships, jobs, and on and on. I learned a lot about my adult life and how I had been living with mild signs and symptoms of bipolar disorder for several years. Nothing too interesting from my adolescent or teenage years presented itself. It was all about my adult life. The doctors took one look at my pattern of short-lived jobs and repetitive moves around the country and tied those events to changes in my mood that I had not recognized over the years.

It became very obvious soon after beginning to analyze my life that I had bipolar disorder. Once the doctors and I had the big picture in front of us, there was just no room for doubt. Throughout this process in the hospital, I drew in my journal my own timeline of major life events along with my accompanying prevailing moods over the years. I made the graph as a way to cement the diagnosis into my mind. But that wasn't even necessary because it was all so crystal clear.

So many friends visited me in the hospital. Jill, a friend from college, brought me a journal. I wrote a lot of strange notes in the journal over the week. I recall having the feeling that I needed to write a book about my experience and that journal was the beginning of me becoming a writer. Prior to that journal all I had written were songs.

Many other friends visited as well. I felt lucky to have so many visitors. There were about 10 friends who visited over the week, plus most of my family. I could tell that the other patients in the hospital were a little jealous, as many seemed to not have a single person in their lives.

My parents brought me a National Geographic magazine and it had a tear-out poster of Africa. I hung the poster up on the wall of my hospital room for the week. It reminded me of a person who I gave flight training to who had a business doing African fly-in safaris, which reminded me that I was on an adventure, whatever was happening.

I actually enjoyed being in the hospital. But given my euphoria, I would have enjoyed being anywhere at the time. The bad news of receiving the diagnosis of bipolar disorder felt like good news. It felt like I finally had answers about why I was so restless in my life, about why I couldn't stay in one place for very long. Receiving the diagnosis felt like someone told me that I had a bone fracture in my foot and that I better be careful how I walk. It was also like I had been given the missing puzzle piece.

It didn't hit me very hard while I was in the hospital that I wouldn't be flying anymore. I felt too high on life to be concerned about not flying, almost like I didn't believe it was true. Maybe that was a form of denial. Or perhaps I was just too distracted to accept the reality of the situation. I was grounded, but I was too happy to care.

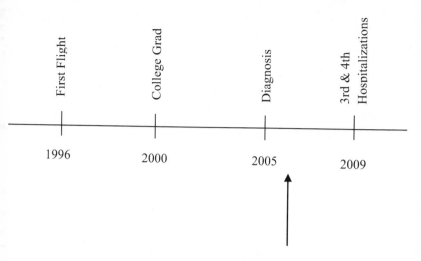

## Chapter 12: Year One After Diagnosis

- Minneapolis, MN - October 2005 to July 2006 -

- Ages 30, 31 -

- *In the Moment* & Looking back -


       Lithium took over my life after I was diagnosed in the fall of 2005, and it kicked my ass. I didn't understand why it wasn't working well for me. I was told that lithium was the most commonly used mood stabilizer for bipolar disorder. I admit that it did keep me far from manic. But it made me feel drugged, slow, and numb. Maybe the dose was too high. Maybe it just wasn't the right drug for me. But that's what I was on for that first winter after my diagnosis.

       For the entire winter I did not do much. I delivered furniture for eight hours a day, came home and ate dinner, ate a bowl of ice cream, read, and went to bed. I almost never hung out with any friends. I wasn't overly depressed, given the circumstances. I had the motivation to go to work full time with an arrival time of 6:00 AM. I was doing OK. The fact that I could no longer fly haunted me and I tried not to think about it. But I quickly learned that the sight of a jet in the sky could bring me back into the cockpit for a few seconds, just long enough for someone to tell me to get right back out. It was difficult to not see the reminders flying overhead.

In April, 2006 I was still living with my parents in friendly Fridley, Minnesota. My medications had recently changed and I was feeling better…no more lithium for me. The clouds had begun to part. The snow piles began to disappear. Still delivering furniture, I appreciated the fact that there was no more ice on the walkways and doorsteps. There were signs of hope. Winter was over and something better would follow. Anything would be better than the previous seven months of lithium and cold.

I couldn't believe it was finally April. The winter took so long to run its course. I didn't drink over the winter and that didn't seem to work any miracles, so I figured maybe it would be ok to have some drinks once in a while. I thought it was probably time for me to hang out with my friends more often, and I finally felt like doing that. That would be a good change. The best change though, and at the same time the worst change, was my medication.

On a different mood stabilizer that spring, I felt different. It was like I had been wearing sunglasses all winter long indoors without knowing it and someone unexpectedly pulled the glasses away from my eyes. It was like I had been driving an old rusty truck through the fog, uphill, with a full load and a heavy trailer in the middle of the night, and then I began cruising downhill on a fast motorcycle on a clear sunny day. Everything was getting better. Delivering furniture eight hours a day was getting easier. I wasn't crazy about it, but it still seemed like a pretty good job. I was enjoying the contact with the customers and meeting new people. The fact that I couldn't fly didn't matter as much then as it did during the winter, but it still hurt. I still felt cheated.

Without any awareness at the time, I started having increased energy and activity throughout the spring and into the summer. The classic signs and symptoms of mania began to kick in that spring. I had increased energy and decreased sleeping. At some point I started partying and drinking again.

Very common in mania is a drastic increase in sex drive often accompanied by promiscuity. I experienced both of these. There were two women I became involved with in the spring and summer of 2006, both for very brief periods, one for just a night. I understand why this subject is one that is not discussed much. It's embarrassing. It's not like me at all to have a one night stand or become sexually involved with a woman almost immediately upon meeting, but that's what can happen when a person with bipolar disorder becomes manic.

The excessive spending and financial troubles that are often part of mania is something else that I experienced in 2006. For one, I spent about $21,000 on a new motorcycle and new riding gear. I couldn't afford a dime of it at the time. But it was an incredible bike and riding it was the closest I've come to flying without leaving the ground.

Another example of financial problems was a shopping experience I had at a book store. I went in and within a matter of 10 minutes, I had picked out and purchased over $250 worth of books. What was I thinking? I just grabbed whatever I wanted and bought it without thinking about it. I had no care about money at all. It just didn't matter. It ties into the way I have handled money since I graduated from UND and moved to Spokane. Throughout all of my moves around the country, I never gave a thought as to what the moving would do to my bank account. I just picked up and moved because I wanted to. I had credit cards and I loved using them. I wonder what it cost to move from…North Dakota to Massachusetts to North Dakota to South Carolina to North Dakota to Washington to Alaska to Minnesota to Florida to Minnesota to Florida to Minnesota to South Dakota to Oregon to Minnesota to Washington and finally back to Minnesota.

As the spring turned into summer, I wasn't aware that I was getting really manic. It seemed to hit me out of nowhere. I had some time off from work and had been camping for nearly a week by myself at different state parks in northern Wisconsin. On my way back to Minneapolis I saw the exit signs for Eau Claire, Wisconsin. I exited and found my way to a city park, Rod & Gun Park, alone. I went to the park because I was on a mission to visit my past, revisiting the first memory I have of experiencing change. The memory comes from the age of about nine or ten, between the fourth and fifth grade. My family lived in Eau Claire, Wisconsin at the time, and my dad had just accepted a job in Minneapolis. We were about to change. My mother took my brother, Kevin, and I to the store where we bought toy plastic boats with electric motors and props that actually worked. Then we were off to Rod & Gun Park, playing in the small ponds with our boats. It was a celebration of things to come. But what would come next? I didn't know what was happening. We celebrated change. I loved the idea. I consider my first important life lesson to be that experience, that openness to the idea of change and the willingness to accept the idea of the unknown, embracing it to the point of celebration.

In my spring and summer mania, I thought I would need to make a documentary film about my life to explain to the world what it is like to have bipolar disorder and especially what it is like to be manic and understand the universe and know God. I had my truck packed with video equipment, although more than anything, I thought I had most of the filming done and all that was left to do was to edit all of the videos I already had.  For years I had been in the habit of taking video of myself and my friends wherever I would go.

So, at Rod & Gun, I got manic and realized I had my video camera and thought that I had stumbled upon the most unique of all opportunities in the realm of documentary films. I got my video camera out of my truck.  I was in the parking lot of the park.  I began filming.

## Video Description – In the Moment – Pressured Speech and Flight of Ideas

*As I write this next section, I'm watching the video that I shot while I was manic at Rod & Gun Park.  This transcription from the video will likely seem chaotic and lack any sense, but that is the point of sharing it.  Note that Sarah in the rest of this chapter is a friend, not to be confused with my wife Sarah.*

I see myself.  The camera must be in my left hand, the shot coming from the area of my waist, almost in front of me and pointing right at my face.  I have a cell phone jammed between my right shoulder and my right ear and I am talking, talking fast, really fast.  I'm on the phone with my friend Sarah.  I am talking her ear off.  I can't seem to stand still.  I am holding two HI-8 video tapes in my right hand and I am pacing around aimlessly.  The view from the camera that is down around my waist captures my face and the treetops above me. My mouth is yapping away incessantly.

I say really fast and non-stop to Sarah. "...ummm, would you...let's see, what's going on here? Oh, this is crazy. I get it, I get it, I, I know I get it. That's why it's crazy. It took me one time. I did it once and I learned it and that's the way I've learned my whole life. Which is, ahhh, it's one time. I can totally teach people how, I can teach anybody anything, and I can teach anybody anything because I know I can learn anything and if I can learn something, then I know how not to learn it, then I can teach it. Alright, the next step... Sarah?"

Sarah says "Yeah," nothing more.

I continue, "This is important...this is important. Ok, I'm getting this one. You have to, ahhh, OK, I'm gonna do a quick run-down on the, uhhh...journal that, that I wrote. Guess what? Just so you know, I'm hiding all of my, ummm, well, I only have one, two, and then one that works the door. I'm hiding my ignition keys."
Sarah says "OK."

Obviously, I am not making any sense. All of a sudden I am leaning inside my truck door, the phone still held by my shoulder. I set the video camera down on the driver's seat and although I am not clearly or entirely in the picture, I can make out that I am leaning towards the extended cab of the pickup behind the front seats. I have my keys in my hand and I remove a plastic cover that is over the car-jack and I put

121

my keys in there. That is where I am hiding my ignition keys. I'm trying to hide them from myself.

I continue, "I told you that before, but this is interesting."

Sarah offers a short, but unintelligible response.

I say, "No, I'm not gonna tell you this time and that's the interesting part because I had two different motives and the first one was because I had an urge to drive my truck and then I said, well I want those keys out of my face because they are making me want to, uhh, drive….the truck, and now what am I looking for?"

The camera tips over on its side as I walk away from the truck. All I see is a view from inside my truck which is looking at the opened door with the trees of the park in the background. I am nowhere to be found, but I can still hear myself, so I must be close.

I say "OK, now this is crucial. I have to write this down now, or I will never remember and it won't be part of the movie. I can't believe I just said that. I, no way, it's,…OK, where, uuhhhggg, where is that fat-ass journal that I wrote in while I was in the hospital? There it is. Oh my God, this is unbelievable! I can't believe I figured it out. That was on September. September…what is it? I'm not gonna turn my ignition…oh God, I can't believe I keep not turning that thing on."

I see my left arm swing into the picture and then it is gone.

I continue, "OK, I think I just realized I don't have to write those, uhhh...., six. I gotta find this now. I'm totally doing two, three things at one time and I'm not doing them, like, uhhh, what would you say? Not doing them, uh-oh, I got a fucking blank...but is it blank?"

I still only see the sideways view of the opened door from inside the truck. In the background is the sound of a car pulling into the small parking lot.

I say, "OK. So, I don't need to write those six things down because they are so important that I keep coming back to them and all is do is get mad at myself for not coming back to them sooner. Ummm...think think think think think think think. So, this is crazy that, this is, this is, this, this is gonna be, ahhh, I can't even believe it. I have to do something before I get to the journal. 'Cause I'll get to the journal for sure because it's only gonna get more...I gotta quit talking without the recorder on. Ok, it's a small recorder. It was in a white plastic bag. I took it out and put it all in one spot and it was right here and now what we're doing...this is funny. I should not procrastinate because I've procrastinated, ha!...how ironic?, procrastinated, um..., on the uh...labeling any type of media, umm..., Vancouver, oh that one's labeled. Probably use the ones that...this is a start. I'll probably, well, oh damn I need to not walk away from this recorder. Alright, I gotta find home base here. I'm gonna make it the hood. And I'm not gonna move as soon as I get everything over here and I'm just gonna put it all over here and, about, what I think is about a minute and you tell me when I say I'm done with my minute, your're gonna tell me how long it was and I'm guessing your're gonna say when it's done, it's been about 23 seconds. OK, go…, and…stop. How close was I? It was what!!!??? It was three seconds!!! Ok, that's three seconds to 60 seconds. I'm sure they know this part. This isn't exactly difficult, right? Three…three to 60, so one to 20. OK, how close are you?"

Sarah responds, "I haven't even left yet."

I say, "I don't believe you. Are you serious? Oh yeah, I do believe you because…"

Sarah says, "I'm waiting for someone to come with me."

In the background is the sound of another car pulling into the parking lot.

I say, "…OK I just totally tried to play casual and apparently I am not an actor 'cause the people just drove by and I'm thinking that they think I'm manic and that's gonna be interesting to see for myself…is what do I look like and sound like right now…like I feel like I'm shaking right now. I'll tell you what I feel as I do it. God, now that I uhhh…..alright, this is the deal, this is the deal. Ummm….oh hey, I'm gonna call a locksmith, well, 'cause I'm throwing my keys away. OK, so, it's all gotta be on tape and I'm going to record and play at the same time because…I'm shaking now, I can see it, so I know that will be on the movie. I just started to say out of the ear shot of the recording devices, that you, when you get here…will be wanting me to go immediately. I am, I am, I am now speaking the same way I hear myself speak when I write. God, this explains a lot. Oh my God! I'm blown away! This…you know what though? This is awesome! Last Fall, when I had that severe manic episode…..there's two main things different now. On my second one, I've done so much work…September…It was in September, October, November, December, January, February, March…that was March…oh my God, it's all frickin' perfect. Alright, so I'm just gonna list some…let's see…list some names….February, March, April, May, June, July…11 months? Ten or 11, I can't remember right now. I have it written down in my journal right here that I'm gonna read tonight. Oh, Sarah…I started to ask a long time ago, and this is also gonna sound interesting that I just came back to it…I want to know later when I watch it…., I want to know how long it's been because, ummm, it's fucked up. You're not even gonna get it. Oh I want you to… I need you to stop and get, ummm, Hi-8 tapes, like digital-8, Hi-8 tapes, please, uhhh get a shit load. God, ya know what? How crazy too!"

## After Watching the Video

I had to stop the video. I had held onto that video tape for the previous three years trying to build up the courage to watch it. It was locked in one of my small, fireproof safes for those years, as it will probably remain. After seeing myself so manic, talking so fast, bouncing from subject to subject, and so full of myself, I just had to stop the video and take a break. I did get back to watching the rest, all 60 minutes of it. It goes on, covering when the police show up to take me to the hospital. As was mentioned in chapter one, the camera was even rolling when I asked the police to hand-cuff me.

After the police took me to the hospital, I had another medication change. Things settled down. I stabilized. Finally, it seemed that I might be headed in the right direction with my treatment.

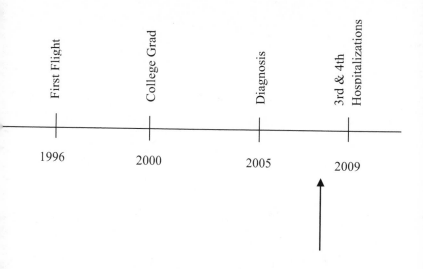

## Chapter 13: Three Years of Stability
- Minneapolis, MN – 2006 to 2009 - Ages 32 to 34 -
- Looking back -

From August 2006, I was fairly stable until February of 2009 at which point I began a major medication change with the idea of avoiding the likely long-term side effect of developing diabetes. The medication change caused sleep disturbances which became part of the equation leading to mania. For my entire life, I have battled poor sleep. I've always been a night person, preferring to sleep in during the morning. Losing sleep is usually the first sign for me of getting manic. If I have little sleep coupled with high energy, I start to get very concerned. If my sleep becomes too poor for too long I will likely become unstable and my mood can shoot off into either direction, although more likely mania than depression.

I refer to these years as stable because I was able to live my life without seriously affecting my ability to function as a person is expected to in society. I held onto my job with the furniture company, and continued to be a great employee, never straying from my focus to do a good job at work. I certainly did not view my job as a passion, and eventually I made plans to try to get into grad school for social work, but while I pursued this new goal, I continued to work successfully.

Beyond maintaining work, I consider these years as stable because I was able to maintain and improve certain relationships. During these years I started dating the woman who is now my wife, Sarah. We also got married during these stable years. It was a success for me to maintain this relationship.

Also, I was not drinking and partying. There was a very rare glass of wine or beer here and there, but I had finally realized that alcohol and medication just didn't mix well. I had a pretty good focus on exercise and started to eat a little healthier too.

Despite holding onto the idea that these years were stable, I still experienced disturbing thoughts. I have kept several journals over the years with the idea that it is part of my wellness maintenance. Doing so allowed me to let those disturbing thoughts out of my head, and also allowed me to back to them later and try to make sense of them. Overall, it has been a way for me to monitor my moods. I'm including some of my journal entries here from my stable years.

## Selected Journal Entries From 2007 to 2009

### June 3, 2007 10:46 AM

*I'm feeling manic, just beyond the beginnings of mania. I am restless. I hate the city right now and want to be in Montana or Washington, very much in northern California. Tomorrow is the anniversary of my sky-dive. I am restless. I have today and tomorrow off from work. I am trying to chill. I need to figure out what to do today to chill. I might go to a movie even if Sarah doesn't want to go. I may go by myself. I kind of want to swim, maybe go to the cabin. I am restless.*

### June 19, 2007 5:24 AM

*Looking to my right are open windows, just slightly open, three stories above the ground. To the left is love. Behind me is a place to make myself clean again, and in front of me, the door to anywhere. I was lost two years ago, terribly lost. And now, I am in the middle of these choices and I like it here. Two years ago, I would have bolted for that door in front of me and left, headed anywhere, far away. Yes, anywhere would do just fine. Two years ago I would not have turned to my left because I knew love wouldn't make me happy. I could have love, but it was not part of the solution to my problems. I'm not sure how I knew this. Two years ago I would not have moved to my right towards the open windows, because they would only tease me, and if I took a quick look I might jump out and smash into the ground. Two years ago I would not have turned around to see what was behind me, the place where I could once again get clean. I had already been there and it fucked with my head. And now, in the middle of all these choices, I sit still and appreciate these options and consider that they are there if I need them. I'm OK here because in a few minutes love will wake from my left and say good morning to me. The windows to my right will shine with the sunrise. Behind me, I will soon wash and get ready to move out the door in front of me. I don't need to use any of the choices, but I will use all of them. Maybe that is the difference. I know what they are all for.*

*June 30, 2007 5:44 AM*

*I just woke up feeling the power of the days I used to live, the days when I woke to the thoughts of taking off in an airplane and heading west across the Rockies. I miss that feeling. Now I wake to a routine of two rushed cups of coffee, a quick bowl of cereal and hopefully a shit somewhere in there, all before I have to throw on my dull work clothes and head out the door* to another day of unloading semi truck loads of furniture and not doing much more than unwrapping that furniture, inspecting it, and rewrapping it so that the next day the furniture can be delivered. It's such a crock of shit that I have to remember the feeling of the life I used to live. I want it back.

### July 4, 2007 at the cabin

Geese in a row, five to be old.
I never knew my heart would be sold.
Fix all the stables, tear down the trees.
The fish have it made to be lost in the sea.
Dragon fly flitters as I dream of when,
Never could never be an option.
Five to be old are startled away.
I watch them go and they have it made.

### September 12th 4:43 AM

Yesterday at work, I went to an emotional wellness meeting at work with a speaker by the name of Joy, a life-coach. I want a career similar to hers. I want to help others. I need to help others. In the meeting there was a woman who I work with and I don't know her name but she was crying and she seemed to be a wreck and she seemed to need help and I want to help *her, but I don't know how. And I think I probably shouldn't even try to help her because she is in my work environment.*

*I got Joy's business card and talked with her about maybe working together to support some of my emotional struggles and she said she thinks she could support me, so I MUST call her.*

### *November 02, 2007 4:37 AM*

*A dream from last night.....*

*The devil, red, appeared before a crowd of people, small child, was he me? A guy was there with a kid. It was like I knew who they were, but at the same time, I didn't. The boy in the crowd turned red. The devil showed up and he was red and he said something to the boy in the crowd, a young boy – almost seemed like an innocent baby but was a little older maybe two or three years old. The devil said something like "You, yes you, they told me I would find you here." And the devil approached the boy and the boy was drawn to the devil and the boy was lifted up by the devil and the boy liked it, he liked the devil, he was being picked up by the devil as if the devil was the mother of the boy – picking up the boy to love him. But the boy was clueless.*

*Non-dreams.....*

*I met with my life-coach Joy yesterday for our third meeting. I didn't know why I was there. I felt numb and confused and*

*felt like I was wasting my time and money and* ~~was~~
*was not really good at what she was supposedly*
*she was good at. I was sad. I talked about my* ~~r~~
*tests done for possible cancer and about how I* ~~c~~ *........ried*
*for my family. My thoughts were scattered and my mind felt*
*blank. I wandered into stuff about forgiving my parents and*
*forgiving myself for holding things against my parents. And I*
*talked about how my friend Brooks called and said he was*
*flying again. Then my friend Tory called and said she was*
*going back to flying at Mesaba Airlines and there was a flood*
*of emotions from aviation memories. I started to cry.*

### *November 13, 2007, 9:14 PM*

*I can't sleep. I feel like I am going crazy. I am having my*
*video flash floods of the mind. I am kind of fucked up. I don't*
*want to go to work tomorrow. I want to quit. I would like to*
*go back to school full time, but I am afraid of doing that. I*
*don't know why I am afraid. Why am I afraid? Why am I*
*holding myself back? What is the worst that could come from*
*me going back to school full time? Why am I still at my dead-*
*end boring job? Who am I? What shall I be? I still think it*
*would be great to be an author, working with the freedom of*
*my own schedule. I am not sure if I could be a journalist, or a*
*columnist. I don't know how I would react to having the task*
*of writing about a certain subject, as in an assignment. I am*
*fucked. I am afraid that I won't sleep tonight. I do not know*

*I am trying to accomplish with my life coach, Joy. I already feel unprepared for our next meeting, even though the meeting is not for about two weeks from now. My mind is racing. I need to sleep. I need to have a proper shit in the morning. I miss a lot of people. Why are they gone? It's not just missing all the people who were in my life in the past. It's me missing the close ones. And there are so many.*

### *March 17, 2008 5:21 AM*

*I'm back. Last night as I rustled around in bed, I prayed to God that I could get some good sleep. He helped me. Everything is in its right place. What should I do now that I feel OK? Should I start a business? Should I write a book? Should I, should I should I...?*

### *October 6, 2008*

*Four days ago I thought I might be getting a little manic. I was aware of myself and my mind. I felt ill yesterday. I was able to relax last night and I slept well. I am nervous and excited about wanting to get involved with NAMI. I will remain aware of myself and my mind, my actions, thoughts, feelings, and I will take action to keep myself stable and I will make choices, both obvious and difficult to realize, in order to continue my wonderful life.*

*October 7, 2008 11:00 PM*

*I think I need to write a book to myself that covers all of the reasons I have to live. And it needs to cover my real life of who I am and about Sarah and about how much I love her and why I love her. And it needs to be about my family and why I need them and how I know they can help even though sometimes it seems that they cannot help. I am afraid of losing myself, losing my identity or my memory. I am afraid of being hospitalized and really losing my mind. I need a reference to where I am at now so I can have a guide to follow if I need it.*

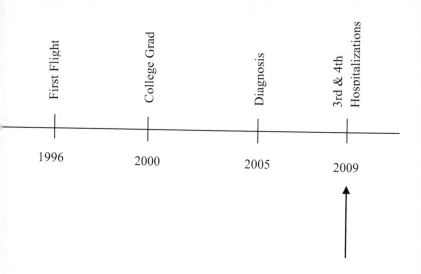

## Chapter 14: Slipping into Mania

- Minneapolis, MN – Spring 2009 - Age 34 -

- Looking back -

**Journal Entry**

*February 08, 2009, 5:25 AM, Three days after being laid off.*

*I'm as free as I want to be. I'm just not sure how free I want to be. I am afraid of losing the safety net of routine and schedule. But I am excited by the prospect of new possibilities. I am confused by how to handle looking for a new job and wanting to go back to school at the same time.*

## The February of My Discontent

Besides poor sleep, there were several other situational factors, life stressors that were in play at the time. February of 2009 really was the February of my discontent. The summary of the month starts with me losing my job on Thursday February 5th, 2009. It was the job with the home furnishing company, the job I started in August 2005.

In the meantime, my father-in-law, Jerry, had been very ill and had been in and out of hospitals and nursing homes. He went into hospice care on February 18th and died on February 21st, 2009. His wake was the following Wednesday and the funeral on Thursday. I was a pallbearer at his funeral.

Back in January, prior to being laid-off, I had submitted applications for graduate school at two different nearby colleges, each for a Master of Social Work program. On the day of my father-in-law's wake, I received a letter from one program notifying me that my application was denied. The day after Jerry's funeral I received a letter of denial from the second program. I cried a lot in February, more than I ever have in my life.


## Winter and spring of 2009 – Medication Changes

My psychiatrist and I agreed on some major medication changes which started in January of 2009. It seemed like a good time to make some changes. My doc and I planned this last fall, thinking that I should get through the potentially stressful holidays before changing up the meds. Thanksgiving, then Christmas...too much family time makes me cranky. It was a good idea, but it didn't pan out the way we hoped it would. The purpose of the med change was to avoid the long-term side effect of developing diabetes from a certain medication. The med change was done too quickly, and I started to get manic without realizing it.

## Getting Manic, spring 2009

My sleep was disturbed through March, April, and continued into May and beyond. Over those few months, I slowly became manic, very slowly. If I had been getting good sleep, perhaps my mind could have battled the stress. But that's not how it worked out.

The worst of the stress, for the most part, was brought upon me by myself. In the beginning of April, I had started volunteering with NAMI (National Alliance on Mental Illness), specifically with NAMI of Minnesota's Hennepin County affiliate as a volunteer board member. My first real assignment was to take over the role of newsletter editor. I was excited for the job! But it ended up turning into something that stressed me and, although I let it bother me more than it should have, I eventually had to walk away from the volunteer role.

It all started with me seeking out an article to publish in the newsletter. There was a gentleman who I knew from a NAMI support group in Minneapolis who was getting ready to move to Oregon. Although I didn't know him well, I could tell that he was a very bright individual, very articulate, highly opinionated in a good way, and in general he had a lot to say, most of which I found interesting. I knew that he was a strong advocate for mental health issues and that he took the subject matter seriously. The NAMI-Hennepin County affiliate was going through a major change in board members at the time, and Kyle was one of the members who would soon not be there. Given the situation, I thought Kyle might have something interesting to write for the newsletter. I sent him an email:

*Hi Kyle,*

*Considering your involvement and experience with NAMI, and the fact that you will be venturing west to Oregon, I'm wondering if you'd like to submit an article for the June issue of our newsletter. Perhaps it could be a "farewell" of sorts, focusing on main ideas of what you've learned with NAMI, your experiences in general, goals, and anything you'd like to share, such as a few words of wisdom on how to grow as an organization. Hearing personal stories and advice from "someone who's been there" is always a great way to learn. Please let me know what you think.*

*Thanks Kyle!*

*Brian*

## Kyle's Response

*Brian,*

    *I'm pretty busy getting ready to depart by June 3, AND I think it's a great idea. I'd be honored to write up something. But do know this (and you probably know me well enough to know this already) while the article (how long, by the way?) will be both positive and uplifting, it will also be honest and in places "hard hitting" ..... i.e. the challenges / difficulties with all the Advocacy organizations - including NAMI-Minnesota (and that at times trickles down to us affiliates) being more collaborative and cooperative, and the glaring need for more people - 'consumers,' family members, advocates, service providers, and men in particular (particularly in advocacy and lobbying positions of leadership) to step up and get more involved. On a macro plane Mental Health is in a major crisis in this country, and that includes this state and our county. I would feel a need to at least mention the needs and opportunities ("any good minister and advocate would!").*

    *To not at least mention the major growing edges as I perceive them -- especially since it's partly/slightly why I'm off to a new mental health arena (while it's mainly the Cascade Mountains and Pacific Ocean) -- would be less than candid and honest, and I couldn't do it. Again, lifting up the good (especially here in Hennepin County) would be the thrust, and at least touching on the whole / bigger picture -- most of it fairly good to good too -- would be too.*

*And yes, having this piece be a "farewell of sorts" to my many friends I've served and served with and received so many good things from would be GREAT; so too sharing some of my future hopes and plans, most of them developed around and built on my experiences with our local mental health community right here.*

*Give me a call and let's discuss this,*

*Kyle*


Kyle's first email response had me a little excited. A major part of what NAMI is about is mental health advocacy by way of people coming together, standing up and voicing their concerns and opinions. But there I was, just starting to get involved with NAMI on a local affiliate level, and Kyle was already hinting that if he were to write an article, it might contain a couple swings at NAMI on the state level and perhaps the national level as well. I began to have mixed feelings about trying to get an article from Kyle, wondering if he had some major problems with NAMI that I wasn't aware of. I continued to pursue the article, but it became a source of stress. A few days after our first email exchanges, Kyle sent me his article. I am including Kyle's article, titled *Adios Amigos* in the appendix for two reasons. First, because I care about NAMI and I think this article might help you get a better understanding of NAMI and some of the challenges that exist in the field of mental health. Second, and probably more important than the first in terms of understanding this book, is because this article was the first major subject of my mania in June 2009. I want you to understand where my mind went, and how I went from reality to fiction in my head. When I read this article for the first time, I felt it was beyond coincidence that I was the one who prompted the existence of the article. I deciphered a message within this article to have great meaning on a global scale. My manic creativity paved the way for me to think that I was highly involved in uniting the human race. I believed that Kyle's message was sent from God, and that both Kyle and I were simply instruments of God with a purpose of passing along the message to the people of the world who needed to come together as one and truly live in peace.

A couple main themes stood out to me in the article. One was that of religion, since Kyle talks about his background in ministry and chaplaincy, as well as talk of different churches and their role in mental health advocacy. Another theme was that of crisis. The article touches on the mental health crisis in the United States. Tying together this crisis with the subject of our country's war veterans and their high suicide rate (something that had been covered heavily in the media around this time), my mind created what I believed was a global crisis. I began to believe that the key to stopping the military related suicides was to simply put an end to the wars in Afghanistan and Iraq. That was it! The wars needed to stop, and then all of these problems would go away! It seemed simple to me. I thought...

1) Veterans were killing themselves.

2) If the wars stop, the suicides will stop.

3) The subject of suicide is one of taboo.

4) If we can destroy the stigma around suicide and mental illness, we can admit that there is a problem and a solution.

5) If Kyle's article was read by the world, everyone would easily and clearly see what the problem was.

6) The world would quickly come together as one and realize that world peace was necessary NOW.

7) The fighting would stop.

Putting it all together with my manic and delusional mind, I thought I was holding the message that would stop the wars. I quickly realized that this message was brought to me so that I would take on the task of passing it along to as many people as I could. It became my purpose. In my unrecognized mania, I thought I was a messenger of God. My thought was that I should send it to everyone I know and ask all of those people to send it to everyone they know. I envisioned this message flying around the world at amazing speeds, zipping through cyberspace without any obstacles. With a web of connections, I figured that the message would reach most of the world within a few days, depending on how often people used their email. I was certain that everyone who would read the email would understand the urgency of the message just as I did. It seemed so obvious to me, so simple. The message was perfectly planned out by Kyle. But on a deeper level, I knew the message was the work of God, and that God was simply using Kyle as an instrument to create the message and that after the message was created, God was using me as an instrument of distribution.

I worked hard on Kyle's article, trying to edit it towards perfection. I was proud to be a part of spreading the message within the article. I felt I had a purpose. I felt I had been chosen for this task. I felt special, very special.

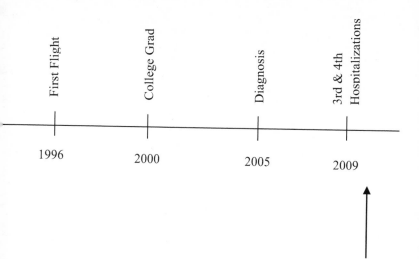

## Chapter 15: In Between Days

- Minneapolis, MN - July 2009 - Age 34 -

- Looking back -

Fairview Hospital looked much better from the outside, but I probably should have stayed there longer. I had done my best to present myself well since I got out of the hospital, but all was not well. Everything that happened while I was in Fairview was weighing heavy on my mind. I still had the strong feeling that all was right with the universe, although at a much lower level. More messages filtered into my head, messages from God. I found strength and encouragement in those messages. I couldn't help but feel that God was leading me on an exciting journey even though I didn't know exactly what that meant. But I did my best to take it easy.

On the first Sunday after getting out of Fairview, while attending a church mass, a very rare event at that point in my life, I received a message from the priest all the way from the front of the church to the back row of the church where I sat next to my wife. He told me in code that I must go and spread the word of God, and that I was to do so wearing sandals.

A gift from God, I've heard people say, receiving messages from God is a gift. I didn't want a gift from God. I just wanted my mind to stop splitting into two. But I felt pretty important being able to receive messages from God. Everything seemed different after realizing that I had a gift that would scare most people. And it should scare them, because it is not a usual experience to receive messages directly from God. It had nothing to do with prayer or having a conversation with God. The messages were one-way, from God to me. I did not ask for any messages or signs from God. Instead, they just started appearing via peoples' voices, through written words, through songs…any type of actual sounds or visual cues that were around me. I was not hallucinating. I was not hearing voices or seeing things that were not really there. I was experiencing what I was told by my psychiatrist is referred to as "delusions of reference." In other words, real voices and real written words were being interpreted by me to mean something different than what the rest of the world thought they meant.

Even though I didn't have a job, I felt like I had a lot going on in my life, mostly because of the volunteering I had been doing with NAMI's Hennepin County local affiliate in Minneapolis. There were two NAMI related events coming up that were on my mind. First, the NAMI-Hennepin County affiliate had their annual summer picnic planned for Friday, July 17th. Second was the "NAMI Walks" annual fundraising event that would be happening in September. On July 16th, the day before the picnic, I went for a bike ride along the same route for which the "NAMI Walks" was planned, a route that started at a park with waterfalls and followed the Mississippi River. This bike ride should have clued me in on the fact that my thinking was very delusional and that I was far from stable, but for those days after getting out of Fairview, my awareness and insight into my state of mind was impaired.

As I biked along the river route, I began to feel very euphoric as the universe was suddenly in complete alignment again. I had felt this before, during my manic episodes in 2005 and 2006, and even just the previous month in June. But this time I thought it was different. Everything really made sense to me, my life, my struggles, the reasons behind my mental illness, the loss of my flying career, and anything that I was ever confused about suddenly had an answer. I brought a notebook and pen with me on my bike ride and I stopped several times to record some of my thoughts. And more important than my thoughts, I wrote down several messages I was receiving from God.

The messages were easy to decipher. They came by way of people around me talking to one another or talking on their phones. I received word that there would be a plane crash at 2:45pm, but I wasn't sure of the date or the time zone or even the location. However, I got a strong feeling that it would happen near where I lived at Lake Calhoun in Minneapolis. I thought about how for years I have had the recurring dream of dying as a result of a plane crash. This made me start to think that I would somehow be involved in the plane crash about which I had received a message.

At one point on my bike ride, I stopped at a scenic overlook of the Mississippi River. As I looked at the massive amount of water flowing by me, I received a powerful message from God about what the "NAMI Walks" would really be about. The fundraising event would be more than just a bunch of people walking. There would be a strong spiritual force behind the event and the water in the river would hold the power and strength of God in order to help attract people to join the fundraising event. There would be a "baptism" of sorts, where everyone who walked along the river would receive a cleansing of their soul and spirit.

Sitting at the scenic overlook, I ran a song through my mind. It was a song I wrote and recorded when I was living in South Dakota at a time when I was experiencing deep sadness and felt like I was going through Hell. The song was a call to God for help and as I sat by the river, I couldn't help but think that this song was written seven years ago for this exact moment in time. The title is "Kill My Thirst." The lyrics are:

*Show me the river,*
*the one that leads to you.*
*Show me the river*
*so I can find my way home.*
*Bring me the water,*
*the cup that kills my thirst.*
*Bring me the water*
*so I can find my way home.*
*Father, bring me water.*
*Let your light be*
*shining out through me.*
*Come on Father,*
*bring me water.*
*Let your light be*
*shining out through me.*
*Show me the people,*
*all the ones who hurt.*
*Bring me the people*
*and I will point straight to you.*
*Teach me a lesson,*
*a lesson in the way to live.*
*Teach me a lesson,*
*and I will cry,*
*cry to you.*
*Father, bring me water.*
*Let your light be*
*shining out through me.*
*Come on Father,*
*bring me water.*
*Let your light be*
*shining out through me.*

Seven years after writing that song, I interpreted it to make sense as I sat along the Mississippi River at the scenic overlook. It was just one more bit of proof in my mind that everything in the universe was in alignment. Everything was happening just as it was planned to be. My life felt important, to say the least.


## Getting Worse

I was the one the world was after. Angels surrounded me, at all times doing their best to protect me from the evil people and souls that were trying to get to me. The angels had their work cut out for them. After I made sense of the evil-doers' plan to kill me, I realized that it was not just their plan that I die, but rather it was God's plan that I die. There would be no way around it. Everything that had happened in my life would turn around and point to me as the target of destruction. It didn't matter what I did any more because any attempt I might make to survive would prove to also be part of the plan that had been in place since the beginning of time. But I did not want to give in, and I decided to use my free will to try to survive. I stayed in tune with what was going on around me and I picked up pieces of their plan everywhere I went.

Carrying with me a small notepad and pen, I walked out of my condo and headed across the street to go to Whole Foods to pick up a couple items for dinner. I had the notepad with me because I wanted to be able to record any new messages I might receive from God. I only received one message on my trip to the store. It happened while I was standing on the sidewalk with traffic flying by as I waited for my turn to cross the street. From my left, down the street and headed my way was a small box truck, all white like an angel's vehicle. I knew that it was part of a message before the truck got to me. I studied the truck quickly, glancing at the license plate and the front of the cargo box, looking for a company name or logo. I didn't see anything. Then as the truck passed me, I saw on the side of the truck the number "7500." There were no other numbers that I could see, or words or pictures. That number was clearly the message.

The number 7500 has a major significance in aviation. It is the transponder squawk code for a pilot to signal a hijacking to air traffic control. I knew immediately that there was a plan for an upcoming hijacking as part of a terrorist attack. I wrote the number on my notepad even though I knew as I wrote it that I would never forget it. Unfortunately, that's all I received for a message, no specific location or time information. Throughout all of my delusions of reference, I was only getting little bits of information. It was frustrating because with my manic state, everything seemed extremely urgent to me, but if I stopped and tried to slow myself down I would realize that any event that I saw or sensed that would happen in the future might not happen for a long time, perhaps years.

## On the Day of the Picnic

I was driving alone to a meeting with a couple other NAMI volunteers and also a man from another local organization. The meeting concerned the GAMC (General Assistance Medical Care). As the NAMI-Hennepin County newsletter editor, I was asked to attend the meeting so I could put some information about GAMC into the newsletter.

I left my home in Minneapolis to drive to my meeting at a coffee shop in St. Paul. Pulling up to the stop light at the intersection of Franklin and Hennepin, before getting onto the freeway, I stopped and waited for the green arrow to make my left turn. I looked to my left and saw an angel running along the sidewalk. She was tall with long blonde hair and a long flowing garment, definitely not something a human would wear. She did not have wings, but she moved swiftly, almost floating around the corner and out of sight in the direction that I was waiting to turn. Immediately, the light turned green, I made my turn and looked for her, but did not see any sign of the angel. I couldn't be sure, but I believed she was one of my guardian angels.

After the meeting at the coffee shop, I was driving to my parents' house and listening to music from my ipod. I felt productive having just gone to a meeting that I believed was important. I had taken a lot of notes and would have a fair amount of organizing to do in order to pass along the information from the meeting to the NAMI-Hennepin County board members as well as to get the information in our newsletter. Thinking about that, it felt like a good amount of stress that would give me something valuable to do with some of my free time, of which I had a lot. As I drove, I felt that everything in my life was falling into place and I felt good about myself. There was a strange mix of normal everyday life duties mixed in with my responsibilities of receiving and deciphering messages from God. I didn't understand the wide array of work that I had in front of me, but I accepted it as the way things were meant to be. I continued towards my parents' place and enjoyed my music along the way. But at a certain point, I no longer enjoyed the music. A song played from my iPod that sent chills through my bones. It was that same evil vibration and terrible electrical current that I have felt before that meant something horrible was in the air. It came from the song that was playing. There was a certain part of the song that was about a mountain named "Monkey." I thought it had to do with the location of Osama bin Laden. I put a lot of attention on that line from the song, but I was wrong about its meaning. I would however find out the meaning of the song in the coming days.


## During the NAMI-Hennepin County Picnic

While at the picnic, I was being watched by angels and a single demon. The angels were there to protect me, without a doubt. The demon was there with the intent on identifying me. I played it cool, never letting the possessed man see me look directly at him. I believed that he had an idea about my super-powers and that I may have been the chosen one, but he was somehow still in need of confirmation. This man, the one I refer to as the demon, I shall call Mr. Dark. Throughout the entire picnic, Mr. Dark followed a man around the picnic area and hounded him for information. The man who was being hounded I shall call Mr. Mouth because he talked a lot. At the time, I believed that Mr. Mouth had a lot of secret information about politics and past wars and that he knew a lot about the truth behind several conspiracy theories.

The picnic ended and everyone was gone, except for my wife and me. I stood with Sarah in the parking lot, my head on fire, my thoughts bursting and spinning, and my mind feeling like it was splitting into two pieces. The race was on again, the race between the two sides of my mind, and there was no stopping now. The mania was in full swing and I knew that the only thing that could stop it was new medication. I had to go to the hospital. There was no doubt about that. There were questions though. First, I had the question on my mind of whether or not Mr. Dark actually left the picnic or if he was waiting for me in his car somewhere, maybe near the park entrance, or across the street from the entrance. I didn't know what his car looked like. Earlier, I had done my best to keep an eye on him so I could cautiously follow him to the parking lot when he left the picnic, with the intention of getting his license plate number, a crucial bit of intelligence. Unfortunately, when he had headed toward the parking lot to leave, I was in the middle of a conversation with my wife and I couldn't figure out how to break away to follow Mr. Dark without making Sarah suspicious. I felt like I had made a huge mistake. I knew better than to let him get away without getting his license plate, but it was too late to fret about it. With the question on my mind of whether or not Mr. Dark was lurking in the distance and watching me, I had to play it cool and act like I was not being watched. I knew that Mr. Dark may not have been there, but he could have alerted others of my whereabouts and the more I thought about it, the more it made sense that I was being watched, possibly by more than one person. I didn't tell Sarah any of this. All I told her is that I needed to get to the hospital. Then there was the question of how I would get there.

Sarah and I had both driven to the picnic, so we had to deal with having two vehicles. My whole family had been there, but had gone home, not realizing the state I was in. Our first idea was to leave my truck at the park and Sarah would drive me to the hospital. Sarah thought we could stop at home first so I could get what I needed for the hospital, but I already had everything I needed with me. All I really needed was my medication and I already had that with me in my truck. I became paranoid about stopping at home, thinking that if the demon possessed people didn't already know where I lived then we might be leading them straight to my home putting Sarah in danger.

Sarah and I decided that we would both drive our cars to our home, leave one car there, and then Sarah would drive me to the hospital. But as I drove, I got too scared about going home. I thought that whomever it was that was out to get me was going to follow us to our home. Then I figured if I were to be in the hospital for a while, Sarah would be at home alone and I didn't want anyone to come after her. In my manic state, I was having a hard time figuring out the way to the hospital, and everything around me felt extremely urgent. I thought that I needed to get to the hospital immediately and I ended up calling 911 while I was driving. At first, I just tried to get driving directions from the 911 operator, but the operator convinced me that I probably should not be driving. I stopped in a parking lot that was actually right across the street from a fire station where the ambulance came from to meet me.

It was all business in the ambulance as far as I was concerned. The paramedics were as calm as me. I could sense they had been waiting for my arrival. There must have been a call out to all of the hospitals giving a heads up that the time was rapidly approaching for me to come in and get direct supervision and protection. Ultimately it was up to me to make the call to come in. I had to play it cool. Despite my racing mind and tight chest and the feeling that my heart would explode at any second, my blood pressure and pulse checked out as normal. I must have been doing a good job of keeping my calm. Trying to speak at a normal pace, I gave the paramedic all of the information he asked for. When asked why I called 911, I told him that I had bipolar disorder and that I had been experiencing "delusions of reference" and that specifically I believed I had been receiving messages from God via these delusions. I explained briefly that I had received information about the current wars and upcoming terrorist attacks, information that was clearly a matter of national security. But I did not tell him that I felt like I was running out of safe places to be, or that I thought people were after me.

I wasn't sure exactly where Sarah was while I was in the ambulance. She may have been driving directly behind the ambulance, or maybe she went at her own pace to the hospital. Either way, wherever she was, I feared that she may be getting in a fatal car accident at any moment. It was killing me that I didn't know when it would happen. Ever since I saw the future when I was in Fairview, I had come to expect that every time she got in her car might be her last time. I felt sick to my stomach as I thought about this in the ambulance. But despite my best efforts to change the future when I was in Fairview, I knew that in the end, grand plans had already been made, and there would be no changing of the future. If what I saw was the truth, then I knew I would be plagued every day as I waited for the future events to occur. Ignorance really is bliss, I thought to myself.

Why would Sarah die in a car crash? I couldn't figure it out. I thought about the idea that maybe we were not really meant to be together. Perhaps my upcoming mission would take me away from Sarah and she wouldn't be able to live with that. I considered the idea that she needed to be with her dad in heaven, and maybe he would sooner or later be returning to take her home with him. All sorts of possibilities popped into my mind. I knew that even if I had seen the future, I did not foresee any knowledge of when the future events would occur, but even with that thought in mind, I couldn't help but feel that everything was urgent and that in order for the wars to end, everything I saw must come true. I couldn't be sure, but although I didn't have specific times tied to events, I was pretty sure that I saw the future events in a chronological order. It all became very confusing and the best way for me to handle it was to try not to expect anything to happen, and instead just try to let events unfold as they were meant to be. But that proved impossible for me at the time.

As the paramedic asked me questions and filled in all the answers on his hand-held computer, I prepared myself for entering the hospital. The most important task I gave myself was to write down some phone numbers from my phone. I figured that at some point soon I would be without my phone and that it would be a lot easier on me if I had a few key numbers at my ready. I copied down my Uncle Greg's number as well as numbers for my friend Blake, my therapist, my parents, Kia, and a few others. I finished copying the numbers just as we pulled up to the hospital, HCMC, Hennepin County Medical Center in Minneapolis.

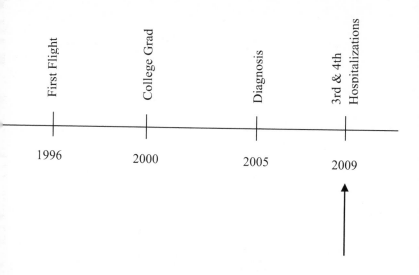

**Chapter 16: HCMC**

- Minneapolis. MN – July 2009 - Age 34 -

- Looking back -

Getting out of the ambulance, I walked with the paramedics to an obscure door, not the main ER entrance. Inside the doorway was a small entranceway with another door that was secure. There was a short old man in the entrance way with two paramedics. The old man was rambling on about something that was difficult to follow. I was instantly sure however, that he had some of the same super-powers that I had. I could sense that this man had also recently seen the future, but unlike me, I sensed that he had been able to see the future for years. He was a prophet. I could just tell. And it was also obvious that he was the type of person you might see walking down a city street talking and gesturing to imaginary friends, looking like a "crazy" person. On a blind judgment, he would probably be viewed on the street as having schizophrenia or perhaps that he was a burn-out from a lifetime of drug abuse. I understood that these quick judgments were likely as I tried to size him up myself, but I knew the truth. He was here for the same reason I was here. He also had information about the wars and terrorist attacks. He must have seen terrible things happen too. This was the moment when I realized I was not alone. And beyond the idea that he also saw the future, I realized he was here because he knew about me. The inside door of the entranceway opened and a woman said "Who's next!" The old man walked through the door with the two accompanying paramedics and the door shut behind them.

As I waited for my turn, the paramedics began an off-topic discussion about the flooring in the entranceway. One of them said something about how he was going to redo the floor of his garage. The floor in the entranceway had a grid-like pattern on it, not in the design, but from some sort of wearing on the floor. The paramedics and I speculated together what it might be from. We agreed that there must have at one time been a large rug on the floor and that perhaps there was a rug pad underneath that, causing the grid pattern to wear onto the floor. It was an unexpected conversation, one to simply kill the silence and the time that had to pass before I could get into the hospital. I pulled my keys out of my pocket and removed a small USB flash-drive that was on one of the key-rings and placed it in a pocket of my backpack. I thanked both men for their help with getting me to the hospital safely. Just then, the inside door opened again, and the same woman was there, this time saying "It's a busy night in the inn. You're going to get the last room."

Before I got through the door, I thought "Of course I'm going to get the last room." That made complete sense to me. I felt like I had a team of people, all with super-powers of some sort, just waiting for me in the hospital. There must be, I thought to myself, a lot of patients who truly are waiting patiently for me to arrive. I didn't know how it would all play out, but I knew something big was happening. I couldn't believe how busy the Acute Psychiatric Services was that night. That couldn't be normal, could it? I didn't think so. The only explanation is that I truly was meant to get the last bed. Someone had reserved it for me. They must have. I wondered for a moment who it was that made that call, then I continued through the door, actually entering the hospital.

As soon as I was in the door, I reached into my backpack and pulled out the USB drive that I had taken off my key-ring. I held it up for the woman to see and I noticed her name tag said Chris. She asked me what that was and I told her it was a USB drive and I asked her if she would keep it for me. It had copies of a lot of my documents, including journal entries, letters I had written to people, emails I had saved, as well as a spreadsheet documenting several text messages I had sent and received. Bringing in the USB drive was a safety precaution. If there was any doubt about who I was or whether or not I was a spy or terrorist, the information on the USB drive would prove vital to maintain both my innocence and the protection I would need to continue my mission.

Chris told me to hang onto to USB drive. I couldn't understand why she didn't want it at first. Then I realized that she didn't need any proof of who I am. Everyone at the hospital really had been waiting for me. They knew who I was. Chris then brought me to a waiting room where Sarah was already sitting, waiting anxiously for me. There were about seven other people in the waiting room.

My mind seemed to calm down as soon as I saw Sarah. My body felt exhausted, like I had been awake for days with no sleep. My brain felt exhausted too. I couldn't tell how long we waited to see a nurse. It felt like a couple hours, but in my manic state I have a hard time dealing with time, so it's hard to say. However long it was, during that time I decided that all I wanted to do was go home and get some sleep. I didn't want to be in the hospital anymore. When I finally saw a nurse, I told her that I had been receiving messages from God. I did not tell her about the evil people who were after me. I didn't tell her about Mr. Dark or that I knew how to stop the wars. Nor did I tell her of my awareness of terrorist attacks that were planned against the United States. I only told her that I had been experiencing delusions of reference and that the messages had stopped, and that I had calmed down. The nurse said that if I felt like going home, I could do that. And that is what Sarah and I did. We went home and got in bed and I tried to sleep.

I awoke the next morning, Saturday, the morning after the NAMI picnic, the morning after calling 911 to get to the hospital. I couldn't figure out how I had arrived at the hospital the previous night and then left and gone home just hours after arriving. It amazed me that the nurse at the hospital knew that I called 911 because I was manic, yet she didn't try to talk me into staying. I'm pretty sure they were just too full of patients in the hospital. Whatever the reason, I was allowed to leave, to go home, to try to sleep in my own bed. But I did not get much sleep that Friday night into Saturday.

On that Saturday morning, I still held the secrets about how to stop the wars and I still felt that I knew the secret information about terrorists and their plans to attack the United States. I knew I had to talk to President Obama. I sent a text message to my uncle Greg and also a text message to my therapist, stating that I needed a secure line to the President. I needed to talk to him, to tell him what I knew. My uncle called me not too long after I sent him the text and said that if I am asking for the President, I should consider getting myself to somewhere safe. Greg knew I was off my rocker. I agreed that I needed to get to the hospital. Then my parents called me. Greg had already called them and told them that I should probably get to the hospital. My parents said they were parked outside my condo.

It was time to go. I quickly grabbed everything I would need for the hospital just as I had for my trip to Fairview the previous month. I took a big breath before walking outside with Sarah. As soon as we got outside, my suspicions were confirmed. Stepping out of our main condo door, from the right I saw an undercover FBI agent walking towards us. We turned left, not because of the FBI agent, but simply because it was the direction we needed to go to get to the street. Before Sarah and I reached the street, we walked between two other condo buildings. Out of one condo walked another plain-clothed FBI agent, and from the direction of the street, yet another agent. I caught only the slightest glimpse of all three of these agents. I knew it would be best if they could acknowledge to their superiors that I had not been acting suspicious of them, and that I seemed to have my act together. The more "normal" or casual I acted, the more likely it would be that they wouldn't have to take me in.

Sarah and I continued to walk toward the street where my parents were parked, waiting anxiously for me to get to them. As we approached my parents' car, I noticed that across the street in the park was a man pretending to use a metal detector to sweep the grass for lost treasures, but I knew he was really an FBI agent and that his so-called metal detector was actually specialized audio surveillance equipment. As soon as I saw him, I looked away. I acted like there was no reason for me to be concerned with him. Without wasting any time, I hugged Sarah and gave her a quick kiss, told her I loved her and that I would see her at the hospital. The plan was for her to drive separately from me and my parents. Sarah absolutely looked concerned and worried. I did my best to comfort her with a look of confidence, reassuring her that I would be OK and that in the end everything would turn out just fine for the both of us. Sarah turned and walked away and I climbed into my parents' car.

At this point, I felt fairly comfortable with being watched, mostly because I knew that the people who were watching me near my condo were on my side. The FBI was clearly protecting me as they monitored my progress towards getting back to the hospital. They did a good job of staying hidden from my parents as well as from Sarah. And of course, I did not tell my parents or Sarah that the FBI was hanging around us. As far as I was concerned, I was working with the FBI and didn't want to cause a scene. The less my parents and Sarah knew, the better off we all would be. So far, up to that point, I knew they didn't have a clue that the FBI was involved.

Making our way to HCMC, the same hospital I was at the previous night, the car was close to silent. I told my parents that I may just need to be left alone for a while in the hospital. As my parents drove me to the ER for my urgent change in medication, I was careful to not look at the cars to my left or right that carried assassins. For my parents' protection, I did not tell them who I really was, that I was special. I did not tell that that I had been chosen to fight the wars. Making it sound like I just needed some room to breathe, I was calm and quiet. My mother told me I was her hero and that she and my dad were both very proud of me and my ability to seek help when I needed it.

We arrived at the hospital and my parents dropped me off at the emergency room entrance. I walked inside and was sure that there were people inside the hospital that were after me. But I also felt that there were people inside the hospital that were there to protect me. I checked in at the desk. The woman who helped me already had all of my information from the previous night, so the initial check-in was quick. She told me to go down the hall and around the corner to the acute psychiatric unit. I could not go alone though. I was too afraid someone might try to abduct me. I asked the woman behind the desk if she would walk with me to the psych unit. She kindly did so. Then I sat in the waiting room of the acute psychiatric unit for a while by myself. My parents were still trying to find parking somewhere and Sarah was still on her way to the hospital.

I was taken to a small room where I would be waiting for an unspecified amount of time. There was a sofa in the room and also one chair. I stretched out on the sofa and listened to my iPod. Chris, the woman who had dealt with me the previous night, came in and told me that my wife and my parents were out in the waiting room thinking that they would be seeing me before being admitted to the psych unit. There was just too much turning around in my head at the time for me to see them. I knew that Sarah was going to die in a car crash soon, and I just couldn't stand to see her at that moment. I knew I was going to lose her and I didn't know how to deal with it. I asked to be alone and Chris left the room, respectful of my wishes.

I kept waiting. Still alone, I just waited and listened to my iPod. My iPod was set to shuffle and I realized that every song that came up in the random order was in no way actually random. Each song showed up just in time, just as planned. It didn't matter what the song was about, whatever song was playing was a song that was written by God to me. I was blown away as I stretched out on the couch and listened, just listened.

I heard a song by Tori Amos called "Agent Orange." I didn't know what it meant, but the song definitely had meaning behind it. It was a peculiar feeling I got. Some of the other songs I heard have made me feel love or on the other end of the spectrum, evil. But this Agent Orange song gave me a different feeling, a subtle "it's going to be ok" type of feeling. I really can't describe it. I just knew the song had meaning, so much meaning that when I heard the song, I was compelled to write down the title on the inside of the back cover of a book I had brought with me from home, "Your Erroneous Zones" by Wayne W. Dyer. I also wrote down the album name, "Boys for Pele." Something made me cringe when I thought of that phrase. I had to document it.

Finally, it all made sense. I wasn't alone in the hospital, not even close. I had all kinds of people with me, on my side. I realized that there was a specific reason why other patients were there. They had all been called to be close to me. They were in the hospital to help me, to support me, and to guard me. I could sense that they knew why they were there, but they were not allowed to talk about it. I was also not allowed to talk about it. I certainly couldn't tell anyone who I thought I was or who I had become. I would have to just be me and be patient with my powers and let the plan unfold as the universe vibrated along its energetic path. Then it hit me that I could be wrong about all of the patients being there for me. I had another idea that perhaps made more sense, one that allowed me to take one tiny step back towards reality. This tiny step brought me down one notch from my high self-centeredness and importance. But I was still part of a special plan.

My idea was that all of the patients around me in the hospital had been having very similar experiences to mine. They must have all seen the future and then gone back in time, then they became God, and then just as I did, they believed they were Jesus. It likely did not happen exactly the same way for each person, but probably in a similar pattern or order. And if this many people in one hospital were having this experience, then it must be happening in other hospitals, and not just locally or even nationally, but it must be happening globally. At that point I knew that all around the world people with mental illnesses were becoming very unstable and experiencing the wonder and mystery of God manifesting in the form of becoming Jesus. What did that mean then? Did it really make sense? There was a problem in my thinking and what I realized next sent me back up a notch away from reality. I couldn't ignore some of the future events that I saw occur when I was in Fairview the previous month. I couldn't ignore that people from all over the world would make an attempt to converge on Minneapolis, to get to the Twins stadium for the ultimate celebration, to attend "The Show," the celebration that I first thought was happening while I was in Fairview.

I continued to wait. After a matter of hours, a young man came into the room and asked if I would like him to pull the sofa out into a bed and put sheets on it for me to sleep. I didn't even know what time it was, but apparently it was time to sleep. And so I slept.

The next morning, in came a woman and a man. The woman said her name was Jeanie. I knew right away that she was a genie. She seemed happy to see me. I was so excited to be in the presence of a genie that although I heard the man's name, I didn't retain it. I immediately thought about my three wishes. I started to doubt myself and my abilities. I wondered if the world really had come to peace already or if I was just still sensing the future. Perhaps, I thought, I needed to wish for world peace, and so I did. I felt comfortable using my first wish so quickly. The other two, however, I would never need to use. The genie checked my pockets and then the man took me to my available room on the psychiatric unit.

An FBI agent, posing as a patient in the hospital unit where I was, caught my attention immediately upon my arrival to the unit. He was playing a banjo when I walked in and he was looking at me, playing me a song. He was there for me. They knew I needed music. There was something safe about him being there with the banjo. When I was hospitalized for the first time in 2005, I was told I could not have my guitar because the strings could be used as a weapon. Seeing the banjo now made me realize that this guy was not really a patient in the hospital, otherwise he would not be allowed to play the banjo or even have it on the unit. I would have sat down next to the music man immediately and listened to his music, but I had to check in at the desk first. The guy who walked me from the temporary room to the behavioral health unit left my side as I approached the desk and was given an opportunity to quietly call out for help.

The woman at the desk asked me a question when I approached. Her first words were "Is this your first *emergency*? She asked the question, hinting that she knew I was in the middle of an international conspiracy and the focal point of many groups of people, and that I was the one who knew how to stop the wars. She was letting me know that she knew what I was going through and that I was not alone. With her first question, she was really asking me to confirm that there were evil people within the hospital trying to kill me. She was an FBI agent. When she asked me if this was my first emergency, I said "Well…it's my first *major* emergency." The woman turned around and looked at another woman behind her. That other woman's face read as if she was now required to pass on my answer, my confirmation that there was indeed a true emergency happening, and that there were in fact people in the hospital trying to get at me to kill me. This second woman looked at the woman at the desk who asked me the "emergency" question, then picked up the phone, looked at me, turned around so I could not see her face, then said two words that I made out to be "he's here."

I realized at this point that she was also with the FBI and that there must be a large group of FBI agents in the hospital with me. And I also realized that they really had been waiting for me, that they knew something miraculous was happening in the world and that there was someone special who was coming to help the world. That person was me, and they knew I was out there somewhere. They had been tracking me, getting closer and closer to me, slowly guiding me to my destination of the hospital where they could protect me.

After I answered the "emergency" question, I was told that I could make only one long-distance phone call that day. I knew what that meant. The woman was trying to tell me to not waste any time. She was trying to tell me to call

President Obama. I knew he was waiting for confirmation from me. The President was hesitant to declare the largest war ever declared, and he needed my word that it was necessary before he would move forward with the required destruction. That meant it was up to me to truly declare war. It would not be easy to make a phone call to the President. With my superior intelligence, I knew that the President made the demand that I not be able to reach him directly by phone. His plan was that if I truly had a message for him, and if I were truly as special as they thought I was, then I would be able to come up with a way to get my message to him. It was like I would have to speak and act in code, letting the FBI agents catch on to what my message was for President Obama. When I was told that I could make only one long-distance call, I knew I had to let them know that I had a message for President Obama. I said "I guess I better make the phone call a good one…make it count, right?" That was the beginning of me asking many questions of the FBI agents and hospital staff. I knew they were there to guide me and advise me, that they really were trying to help me get through this.

After checking in at the desk, I turned around and walked toward the music man, the guy playing the banjo. He told me to sit down and listen. His music was like magic. He said "My name is John. You and me…we're like brothers. Sit down and listen." I knew what he meant, that he and I were soul twins, that in another dimension we would be known as twins. He was my match. John, the music man, had my trust from that point on. Then he said "This isn't a place that you get out of easily or quickly." He must have sensed my urgency.

Across the room was another patient sitting down in front of the TV, focusing on playing his harmonica. He looked at me and told me to sit down. I said to him "I know you from a canoe trip that you took." He just smiled and said his name was Jim.

Let's go back one year earlier. I had been at my grandma's cabin in northwestern Wisconsin. I had taken a ride on my mountain bike and ended up about eight miles away from the cabin at a canoe landing along a river. I got off my bike and took a look around. I approached the river and came upon four older men, all wearing tie-die shirts and looking very much like they lived the hippy life style, long beards and smoking something that didn't seem to be cigarettes. They had two canoes packed with gear and looked like they were on about a week-long canoe and camping trip. One of the men looked at me and asked "Do you have a message from Paul." I had no idea what he was talking about and simply said "No." I turned and left, thinking that the meeting was peculiar.

And now let me take you back to the hospital, back to when I met Jim, the guy who was playing the harmonica. I knew he was the same guy from my bike ride, the guy who had asked me one year earlier if I had a message from Paul. But I soon realized that this guy was actually the soul twin of the guy I met on my bike ride, not the same man in the flesh. Jim played a song with his harmonica just for me. I thanked him for the song, telling him that I needed that. Then I saw the man who would be my primary source of information while in the hospital.

There he was, dressed in all orange, an orange T-shirt, orange shorts, even an orange Minnesota Twins baseball cap. Where could he have possibly found a Twins cap in that color? Obviously, he was Agent Orange. I should have known that he would be there, after getting the strange vibes while listening to Tori Amos' song "Agent Orange" the night before. After seeing him in the common area standing in front of the TV, I retreated to my room and double-checked my notes from the night before. Sure enough, I had documented "Agent Orange" to be something of meaning. It was yet another item on my list of things that were more than just a coincidence.

I'm guessing Agent Orange was about 42 years old. He told me his real name was Eddie. I never got his full story, just bits and pieces as they fell out of his mouth. He was one of the ones that could read my mind. There were at least three others who could read my mind, and another two who I suspected might be able to as well. Eddie was on my side though, so although it freaked me out that he could read my mind, I was put at ease by his friendly demeanor. Most of them were on my side. It was like magic, the way the right people showed up just as I needed them most.

Dr. Harper could not fool me. As I followed him into the small room off to one side of the hospital's behavioral health unit, a man I trusted sat by the door. This guy was the banjo player, the guy who I knew was with the FBI. He sat in a chair next to the doorway of the room I was entering. This FBI agent was dressed in pants that were given to him by the hospital staff. He had a laptop computer that was mounted to a rolling stand. It was a computer that any of the patients could use if they were to ask for it. As I walked by the FBI agent into the room, he gave me a peculiar look and shook his head at Dr. Harper as he said quietly, "Computer...computer." He was communicating with his team via the computer, other agents and important government officials. I would be facing a battle in the hospital. As safe as I thought I would be after getting myself to the hospital, it turned out that several members of the other team had made their way to where I would spend nine days.

I didn't trust Dr. Harper. He was different. He was not like my psychiatrist, the guy I've been working with for five years. This Dr. Harper was not on my side. I knew this before I saw him, before I heard his name. An electrical current and evil vibration had been rushing through my body telling me that someone there at the hospital was trying to get close enough to me to get some of the information I had. It was the same feeling I had in Orlando when my friend Pat and I were close to the guy who fired the pistol. My suspicions about Dr. Harper were confirmed by the music man.

**Bird Team**

While in HCMC, some of the patients who were there to help me often went around the psych unit with a white blanket on their backs. They were angels. They were part of the "Bird Team." They were there to help calm me down and more importantly to help prevent me from escaping the hospital. Every time I started to become too excited, I would hear on the paging-system a voice created by God that said "Bird Team to…" followed by a location in the hospital. The location part of the page was meaningless. The actual call used the word "burn" which was said to disguise the real meaning, "bird." The message meant only that I was getting worked up and that I needed the angels to surround me. And that's what they did. I caught on quickly. I would hear the call, "Bird Team to unit 4 north" and immediately, the group of angels with white blankets on their backs would stand up and walk around me, some of them walking between me and the doors that exited the unit. They were protecting me.

**Monkey**

Let me remind you of the day that I heard the song from my iPod that was about a mountain named "Monkey." called "Fire Coming Out of the Monkey's Head" by the band Gorillaz. When I heard that song I felt with every inch of my body a negative energy that made my bones vibrate with a chill of evil. In HCMC there was a patient who made my body vibrate at what felt like the exact same frequency. For two days I felt this evil anytime I saw this man. The closer I was to him, the stronger the vibration was. On day three, while we were both in the common area near the TV, this man was standing in a trance. He had not been talking to anyone. Then out of the blue, with no obvious recipient of his message, I heard him say "They call me Monkey." I believed this confirmed my suspicions that this man was evil and out to get me. Later that day, this man and I were both in a small room with a group of about eight people for a short therapy session. The staff member who was leading the session asked each of us in the group why we were there. As we took turns answering the question, this man "Monkey" said he was there because he was having homicidal thoughts. I was scared. This only strengthened my belief that I was able to sense people's intentions. As the session ended and the group members walked down the hall towards the common area, another man who I did not trust turned to "Monkey" and asked "How goes the battle?" I interpreted this to mean that "Monkey" was in the hospital for the mission of killing someone and most likely that someone was me.

**Sixth Sense**

I woke with a pounding heart, sweating, gasping for air. My feet were on the floor before I could even think about what I needed to do. I rushed toward the door and went out into the hallway of the psych unit. I hurried towards the staff desk and to my left across the room was a security guard. He was holding his walkie-talkie and without understanding it, I heard the tail end of a transmission. The guard responded quickly, something simple like "Roger...got it" and then he started running down the hall towards the locked unit doors, and with his authority, he was out of the unit. I didn't know what had happened. I just knew that I woke up because somewhere in my mind I knew something happened, somewhere, to someone. I sensed it. I knew that my mind was working on a level that allowed me to sense these things. It was all because I was manic. The mania allowed me to sense these things, and that's where this mental illness is both a gift and a curse.

## Wonder Woman

The battle between good and evil became more complicated. I had a lot of protection in the hospital, just as I knew I would. At first, I had a room to myself, but after waking in the middle of the night because my mind detected an emergency, I told another patient that I needed a roommate and the message flowed through the proper channels. A roommate was brought to me, then another, and another, and the rotation continued. Those roommates were soul twins of people I knew and trusted. Except for Lamonte. I trusted him, but I didn't know his soul twin, not personally, just who he was. Michael Jackson. Michael had just passed away recently, and his soul has appeared in Lamonte. And there he was to help comfort me. Lamonte told me when he showed up on the unit "I just had to meet you man!" He shook my hand and smiled and laughed a secret laugh. But I was confused. Lamonte looked more like Michael Jordan than Michael Jackson, so I debated about who his soul twin was. It didn't really matter. He had shown up to comfort me, and that was all I needed to know for the time being. The same goes for all of the other soul twins who arrived to help me. Take for example the woman who wanted to play ping-pong with me in the recreation room.

During a recreation break on one of the days, as I walked into the recreation room I noticed immediately something of interest laying on the ping pong table which was positioned at one end of a long room. It was a mask of some sort, like an African tribal mask carved out of wood. It was decorated, painted, made to look spooky. There was black and red, and the rest I do not remember. But it was not about the colors. There was something taboo about the mask. There were words written on the mask. One word was "airplane." Another word was "music" and then I saw "guitar." I saw within the painting on the mask a mountain scenery that I was sure I had seen before somewhere in my travels. Looking at the mask made me feel scared. I trembled a little bit inside as I thought someone had decorated this mask for me to see. Yes, I thought, it really was made for me. I walked away from the mask and the ping-pong table thinking that a little distance would help me to settle down, but it didn't help. I tried to change my focus by working out with some weights.

Just as soon as I picked up a set of dumb-bells, in walked an oddly attractive woman, not purely physically attractive, but there was something about her energy that was attractive and maybe even more so I found her to be familiar. I didn't know who she was and could only assume that she was a patient at the hospital, but I thought she may have just as likely been a staff member. She went right to the ping-pong table and began bouncing the ball back and forth with one of the staff recreation room supervisors. They had moved the mask off the table and onto a nearby chair. I felt like I needed to talk to her or spend some time getting to know her or something like that. There was just a really weird attraction towards her. Still feeling scared by the mask at the far end of the room, I asked another staff member if they knew anything about whether or not I was supposed to avoid that end of the room where the mask was. I still felt like the mask was a warning of trouble or a sign that I was supposed to leave something alone. Maybe it meant that I was supposed to ignore my strange attraction to the woman who just walked in. I wasn't sure. But whatever it meant, I knew I couldn't ignore that woman.

I walked up to the ping-pong table and the staff member who was playing with the woman stopped playing and handed me the paddle as if he knew that I was supposed to take over for him. I didn't even say a word about wanting to play, he just handed the paddle over to me. The woman and I said hi to each other. We didn't exchange names because we both knew that our names didn't matter. I could tell at this point that she was a patient. Instantly I realized I knew her from somewhere in my past. I could sense her soul as being a match with someone I used to know, but it was hard to place.

We played ping pong with no questions. After the game, she said "Thanks, I just had to come meet you" as she smiled big. She knew who I really was, not Brian, but the real me, the chosen one, the guy who was saving the world.

Then another patient, a man, said to her, "Hey I know you. You look like Wonder Woman. You're her, aren't you?"

She turned from the curious man and looked into my eyes and said "Your wife is like me."

Then it was time to leave the recreation room and return to the fourth floor. I didn't know where in the hospital "Wonder Woman" went.

**Jerry**

I was let out of the hospital one afternoon to attend a ceremony for my father-in-law Jerry who passed away in February. Five months after his death, his ashes were finally being placed in a mausoleum. I was allowed to leave the hospital with my wife to attend the ceremony because everyone at the hospital knew I was required as a sort of "shuttle" for Jerry's soul to pass into the proper dimension.

187

Jerry and I had a special connection. His soul had been hanging around since his death and it was finally time for him to go home. Luckily for him, the hospital staff was aware that he needed my help. The ceremony was gut-wrenching. Tears flooded my face as the priest talked about Jerry. I prayed for Jerry's soul to travel safely and with confidence. I comforted Jerry's soul through the ceremony. I did my job.

After the ceremony, I went out for lunch with Sarah and her family. The waitress at the restaurant looked and sounded like Whoopi Goldberg and I of course assumed she must be Whoopi's soul twin. Then my wife took me back to the hospital. A heavy weight had been lifted off my chest. I finally felt like it really was time to go home, and I knew it wouldn't be long before I would be sleeping in my own bed. I slept hard that night in the hospital.

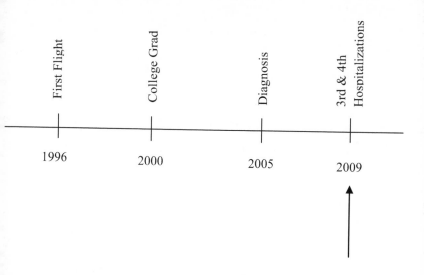

**Chapter 17:  The Landing**

- 2010 -

When I think about how excited I was when I was diagnosed with bipolar disorder in September of 2005, I laugh a little bit to myself because it seems so ridiculous to be happy about such a situation.  My joy about the news of how my brain was broken, having been accompanied by the fact that my pilot career was over, may have been a little out of place. Where was my fear?  Where was my sadness?  That's the beauty of mania.  Anything looks good when mania is in control.  But at the same time, I find it ironic that in the very first moments after receiving the diagnosis, in my manic state of mind, I viewed my situation as I do now, the way it has taken me five years to recognize from a stable viewpoint.  Of course when I was diagnosed, as soon as the mania slowed down, everything around me looked a lot different, and the diagnosis felt like a burden and nothing but bad news. All things considered, the diagnosis has been a lot more than just bad news. It has been a wake-up call.

During my first hospitalization, on my last evening before the day of my discharge, I was let out of the hospital for a few hours. I had stabilized by that point and was all set to go home the next day. For my short break from the hospital that evening, I made plans to meet two friends for dinner, both named Sarah. One of them, Sarah G., is now my wife. I doubt that she remembers this, but when we met at the restaurant that night, the first words from my mouth came out with a lot of excitement and relief. I said "I figured out how my brain works!" That feeling of discovery is still inside me. It is that feeling of discovery that has been the highlight of the past five years since my diagnosis.

The word *discovery* is an important word concerning the topic of mental illness, and it is to be compared with *recovery*. I have a hard time with the word recovery. I believe that recovery is a never ending process and that I will never be recovered. It just never stops. At one of the public speaking presentations I have given on bipolar disorder, a woman in the audience said that she preferred the word discovery over recovery. She made a good point, saying that a psychiatric disorder can provide a person with a great opportunity to learn about one's self and to grow in many ways. Discovery, like recovery, can have no ending. Personal growth has no limit. But I think the difference between the two words is that recovery means fixing something that was broken and simply returning to the starting point, whereas discovery means to change for the better through the experience.

I choose to view my psychiatric disorder as a gift, one which is confusing, but also uniquely beautiful and complete, even if in an extremely complicated way. This gift has allowed me to move toward uncharted territories in my mind and to conquer many of my struggles that on the surface look to be nothing more than signs and symptoms of bipolar disorder.

It's hard to describe how beautiful the world can look when I am manic. Everything is simply perfect. Everything is in its right place when I am manic. I honestly can feel a little sad for people who may never get to view the world from the manic viewpoint. The difficult part about this viewpoint is that it is so wonderful that it is hard to accept as normal. I struggle with the fact that the universe is in alignment when I am manic, but can seem to be such a mess when I am depressed. Of course there is an in-between which is often referred to as being stable, which at times for me can equate to being bored.

I would love for mania to be a choice like a sweet dessert is a choice. Mania is place that a person cannot stay for very long because it is not healthy. But it feels so good. I would love to be able to come home from a stressful day at work and grab a jar of mania out of the fridge and take a little hit to make the pain go away. That would be great if the euphoria lasted for only a few hours then subsided so I would be able to sleep. But once the mania kicks in for me, it seems there is no slowing down, no stopping. There seems to be no control once the mania starts, which means the only thing to do is avoid the mania at all costs. But the problem with that is that it can feel dull to stay away from something that feels so good.

Sometimes I think I would like to be hypo-manic for the rest of my life, just a little manic, not full blown the way I have been before. It seems that the beginning weeks or months of an ascending manic episode can be very productive, social, fun, generally enjoyable, all potentially without any negative effects while it is all happening, until it gets out of control. That is where I want to be all the time. But it doesn't work like that. Instead, I need to take all of the discoveries and use them to live a good life in between the mania and depressions. And I have learned that life can be both stable and wonderful at the same time. I don't have to be manic to enjoy life. It just seems like the easy route. But if I want long-term happiness, I have to take the more difficult route of maintaining my mood, not letting it go where it might naturally want to go.

Life has changed a lot since my diagnosis. My passion of music, song writing, and recording music all seem to have disappeared for five years. The drastic change in my creativity once I started taking medication was incredible. Just recently however, I have felt a new musical creativity and have begun to write songs again. I am learning that I still am a creative person in other ways too. My creativity at this point in life has found an additional outlet, that of writing. I feel it has been a gift, this change in creativity, as I am now able to share a story that may help other people.

As far as my passion of flying goes, it is out of my life. I don't expect flying to return, but who knows. There has been recent progress with the FAA in allowing pilots to seek treatment for depression and not be disqualified from flying. I don't know if things will go so far in that direction to include bipolar disorder, but maybe, just maybe, someday the stigma will be reduced enough for that conversation to at least begin to take place.

Receiving the diagnosis forced me into a situation in which I was uncomfortable and it made me take a close look at myself. Bipolar disorder made me figure out who I am and what it is that I want from life. It also brought out the best in relationships that had a lot of room for improvement. I am now closer to the members of my family because of bipolar disorder. The struggles we have gone through with the difficulty of communicating about the illness have forced me and my family to break through barriers in order to maintain our relationships. Things had to get worse before they could get better.

And things really have gotten better in several ways. Despite having bipolar disorder, I live a great life. My wife Sarah and I started dating a year after I was diagnosed, a year after I told her that "I figured out how my brain works!" The timing of my manic episodes did not allow her to see me completely unstable until June of 2009 when I went into Fairview. It has been difficult for her to try to understand this illness, but we are working through it and making it work. It's very possible to have a healthy marriage despite having a psychiatric disorder. After a lot of thinking and talking about the subject, Sarah and I even decided to have kids, and our first baby is on the way as I write this. I know that a lot of people will think that a person with a mental illness should not have kids, but I cannot let myself take too many opinions too seriously. I have to live my own life the way I feel it should be lived.

The transition from that last hospitalization in HCMC into the real world was far from smooth. In fact, I dropped into a deep depression in the fall of 2009, as deep as the depression that I experienced in Vancouver, Washington, in the early part of 2005. I made a plan for suicide that I only fantasized about, never taking any action on the plan. Fortunately, I was surrounded by people who loved me, and I got the care I needed.

In the spring of 2010 I accepted work as a gardener for a small gardening company, Bluebird Gardening, in Minneapolis, and at the time of finishing this book, I am still employed with that company. Similar to working for the furniture company over the recent years, my new job as a gardener has been far from flying and far from working in a recording studio. But things are different at this point. My goals have changed. I want a job that is close to home and one that has a fairly routine schedule. As I began my new job, I learned that I really enjoyed working outside. I have also worked on the company's book-keeping a couple days each week, and that gives the routine a little shake, just enough to prevent the job from feeling like too much of the same thing every day. And to top it off, I benefit from the flexibility in my schedule which allows me to do public speaking, telling my story of living with bipolar disorder.

I don't want anyone to get the idea that I am cured of my difficulties with bipolar disorder. A person might look at my life and see several good things such as the fact that I am able to hold down a steady job, the fact that I have several important relationships in my life, that I am in a great marriage, that my wife and I will be having our first baby soon, that I have learned many ways to take care of myself, that I have the will and energy to volunteer and make a difference in the lives of many people, and on and on. I have created a great life for myself. But I can't let my guard down. I know better. And to say that life is perfect would be a lie.

I choose to be positive about my losses. Bipolar disorder has made me a better person. It has brought people in my life closer to me, and also me closer to them. I have broken through many of my fears because of the psychiatric diagnosis. Because of experiencing bipolar disorder, I have learned how to stay in one place, to commit to a job, and even more important, how to commit to one person. I have learned that I can be passionate about life even if I don't have my passions of music and flying. In the end, I am thankful that I have been brought down to earth by this disorder. I really have been grounded by bipolar disorder, in the sense that I have found new stability in my life. Even when things get a little rocky, I hold onto the idea that I am no longer lost in the clouds. I hang on to the feeling that I have finally landed.

# Appendix

Here is the article from the NAMI-Hennepin County June, 2009 newsletter that played a role in my manic episodes of that summer.

"Adios, Amigos"

by Kyle Kneen

This will sound like a cliché, but I truly AM honored to be asked to write a farewell piece for the *NAMI-Hennepin County Connection*. I've been on the Board of Directors and a participant in the Consumer Support Group for over two years, and by the time you get this I will have departed for a new life in the Pacific Northwest.

Exactly four years ago, I found myself mired in a paralyzing clinical Depression.....complete with thoughts of suicide. I had moved back to Minnesota two years earlier to care for my mother with Alzheimer's (she having been part of NAMI for almost 25 years). She died within six months and I suddenly inherited my father to care for (not the original plan at all). That went very poorly, and in June of '05 I checked myself into a local hospital. That two day experience also went very poorly, but did get me back on lithium (32 years total now) and connected me with a superior counseling clinic attached to a large church which helped me onto the road to recovery and wellness. My "resurrection day" - the day I knew the Depression had finally lifted - was Christmas Eve 2006. So now Christmas is also my personal Easter.

Shortly after that I joined the Mt. Olivet Task Force on Mental Illness (now renamed The Mental Health (M.H.) Task Force) and started attending NAMI groups and events and then joined the Board. This then led to an immersion into the Twin City Mental Health Community (advocacy and support) - city, county, and even state. At one point I found myself serving on seven boards, councils, and a think tank. Of all of them, I've considered NAMI-Hennepin County to be my anchor and base of operations. I would humbly and strongly consider all of you reading this to step up your participation and involvement with this organization -- perhaps taking it to the limit.....serving on the Board of Directors. I'll share honestly that it worked out great for me.

I've just started writing a book: "Have Lithium, Will Travel." The subheading is "Unusual Escorts On An Odyssey From Brokenness Towards Wholeness." I throw that in now because I believe Relationships (our escorts on the journey) are what life and our recovery are all about. And I'd like to pause now to lift up ten individuals I've met on this Minnesota journey as colleagues and friends who have been key. I'm calling them my personal top ten (a la Letterman) in the local M.H. community, and those of you who know me well, know what a sort of stickler I am for parity between men and women.....so this list is half and half.....

David Eckholdt, Michelle Palmer, Lee Brandt, Jennifer Paddleford, Kurt Froelich, Jill Ann Marks, Bruce Weinstock, Jan Miriam Buntz, Andrew Gadtke, and Theresa Carufel. (Also, Drs. John McClay and Ron Groat - simply the best!)

Together this group's involvement spans MHAM (M.H. Assoc. of MN), NAMI, CSN (Consumer Survivor Network), the Barbara Schneider (CIT) Foundation, The MN Dept. of Human Services, SAC (State Advisory Council & Subcommittee on Local Advisory Councils-LACs), Henn. Co. LAC, INMH (Interfaith Network on M.H.), Mt. Olivet M.H. Task Force, various support groups (family and consumer), and The Northern Lights Social Club -- a new consumer grassroots organization focusing on mutual support and fun. Several of these individuals almost run the gamut of everything listed above on their own - and are thinking of adding more - truly amazing!!

Several members of this groups also served as presenters on a panel on "Mental Health Ministries" (which also contrasted spirituality and religion) that former Board President Brian Marcum and I put together in the spring of 2008 for a Friday NAMI educational gathering.

A number of these folks also served on a think tank we assembled last year to explore a new paradigm of outreach, modeled after one developed in Scotland: Community Mental Health Chaplaincy. Oh yeah, if you didn't know, my vocational background is in ministry and social work.....preeminently chaplaincy (with a bit of mediation/reconciliation mixed in). Anyway, the thrust of this new community-based outreach is to have professional clergy (accredited chaplains) establish working relationships with hospitals, clinics, institutions (prisons, addictions treatment facilities, colleges, etc.) and develop supportive relationships with individuals being discharged/released and enwrap them and their family with the care and nurture and connections and advocacy they need to thrive rather than just survive in the community (thus preventing re-hospitalization, recidivism, relapse, drop-out, etc). Utilization of BeFriender Ministries (we especially explored the program "Harnessing the Energies of Love"), as well as acting as Connective Liaison to the other key components - Service Providers (hospitals, counseling services, employment and housing agencies), Family Members, Advocacy Organizations, and the Faith Community would serve as cornerstones. Community Cooperation came to be seen as the foundation.

This outreach model was embraced as a great one, but the timing and resources just didn't come together (the nation heading into

a Recession didn't help at all). I wish to thank all those who lent time and vision to this project. Perhaps one day we'll see it or one like it operative in both Minnesota and Oregon. If everything works out just right in Salem/Portland I may try to implement it there (It would be a first in the U.S - come on Twin Cities, beat me out! Really!) If not, another option for me may be Oregon State Hospital - in Salem, where they filmed "One Flew Over The Cuckoo's Nest" (the question being would I be Jack Nicholson/McMurphy, The Chief, Nurse Ratchett, or hopefully the Chaplain or Social Worker - Uh oh). Almost forty years after the movie they're building a
brand new hospital across the street from the old one.

Speaking of the two states, let's expand this conversation to the macro -bigger picture - level: In last month's edition of The Advocate, our national NAMI newsletter, there was an article "Grading and Rating the 50 States on Mental Health Issues." Sadly, there wasn't a single "A" awarded anywhere. Six states received "B's" (New York, Connecticut, Maine, Massachusetts, and Maryland -- one of my old stompin' grounds when I worked for over a decade as crisis chaplain at The Johns Hopkins Hospital in Baltimore, some of it in the psych. wards -, and Oklahoma – Oklahoma?) Both Minnesota and Oregon were given "C's" ....... not so great, but better than most of the states - rated "D" or outright "F." There's *Lots* of work needing to be done in *Lots* of places. The overarching message of this entire magazine, and many other sources, is that Mental Health is in a state of **Crisis** nationally, statewide, and locally.

My two and a half years of involvement in this field have given me some insights, gut feelings, and strong views. Rather than lay them on you, I simply want to say that it's at historical junctions like these that it's even more critical that we all come together, and band together, and work together, and pray together,  and move outside ourselves and our own apprehensions, comfort zones, and self interests. Teamwork and service/servanthood can bring about positive change and personal growth.......Truly, they can.

I would lift up three words and concepts we all need to be promoting and aspiring to:

COLLABORATION     PARTNERING     INCLUSIVITY

And three words and concepts we need to be addressing and letting go of:

TERRITORIALISM
ORGANIZATIONAL/SELF CENTEREDNESS
EXCLUSIVITY

The logo of my denomination, The United Church of Christ, is "THAT THEY MAY ALL BE ONE." Not that the Church doesn't need a whole lot more of that,  but for sure the mental health ARENA -

service providers, advocates/lobbyists, churches, synagogues, "consumers," family members, etc. - needs a whole lot more too. We must persevere to truly come together as a legitimate, authentic COMMUNITY and not just an arena of needs and trials and opportunities. Thus it's up to each and every individual...... that's each and every one of us!                                   ('Thus Endeth the Lesson.')

I'm going to close by sharing some random thoughts regarding language, empowerment, stigmatization, and recovery.

First, I, like so many others I've been in discussion with, hate the term 'consumer.' It's not even a medical or health or healthcare term, it's an economics and business word -- label really. Because of the power disparity it creates/reflects (at least initially) it just doesn't fully serve or help the people it is applied to..... and certainly makes many of us uncomfortable! Still, it is better than just calling us 'the mentally ill.' Alternatives are hard to come by, but insofar as I am a big backer of our needing to have direct involvement in our own stabilization and recovery..... I lean to more empowering, inclusive terms such as 'MENTAL HEALTH PARTNERS'.... or 'Mental Healthcare PARTICIPANTS'....or 'People/Persons who employ mental health services' ("fiscal-ish," but empowering). I also sort of like the term they're using at St. Joan of Arc RC: 'People Pursuing Wellness.'

Also, and needless to say, I disdain that old, worn-out, completely stigmatized and generalized label 'Mental Illness.' We need to put that sucker out of its misery once and for all (Sorry naMI). Likewise, the new one that's more and more appearing on the scene: 'Brain Illnesses' - which may be politically, scientifically, and perhaps even medically correct - but has, to me, a powerlessness/victimization/stigmatization feel to it, especially with its close proximity to mental ILLNESS. I find 'Brain Disorders' a little more palatable, but overall prefer 'MENTAL HEALTH DISORDERS' or 'Mental Health CHALLENGES' or possibly even 'M. H. NEEDS.' This dialogues needs to continue!!

Well, that's about it from me. Come visit me in Oregon - Pacific Ocean, Cascade Mountains, vineyards and lush valleys, covered bridges, (OK, so yes, maybe a few drops of rain now and then), "Ducks and Beavers" (college mascots..... sort of like "Gophers" - all of them a little weird) and hopefully a state advancing in the field of Mental Health and overall quality of Life, just as I see Minnesota and especially the Twin Cities doing.

I'll miss NAMI-Hennepin County.    I will miss you.     Thanks!

Wholeness (Shalom),

- Kyle

About the author:

Brian Jost lives in Minneapolis with his wife and son. His public speaking experience is focused on mental health awareness and education.

You may visit Brian online at:
www.brianjost.com

Contact Brian at:
info@brianjost.com